C-2144   CAREER EXAMINATION SERIES

*This is your
PASSBOOK for...*

Administrative Analyst

*Test Preparation Study Guide
Questions & Answers*

COPYRIGHT NOTICE

This book is SOLELY intended for, is sold ONLY to, and its use is RESTRICTED to individual, bona fide applicants or candidates who qualify by virtue of having seriously filed applications for appropriate license, certificate, professional and/or promotional advancement, higher school matriculation, scholarship, or other legitimate requirements of education and/or governmental authorities.

This book is NOT intended for use, class instruction, tutoring, training, duplication, copying, reprinting, excerption, or adaptation, etc., by:

1) Other publishers
2) Proprietors and/or Instructors of "Coaching" and/or Preparatory Courses
3) Personnel and/or Training Divisions of commercial, industrial, and governmental organizations
4) Schools, colleges, or universities and/or their departments and staffs, including teachers and other personnel
5) Testing Agencies or Bureaus
6) Study groups which seek by the purchase of a single volume to copy and/or duplicate and/or adapt this material for use by the group as a whole without having purchased individual volumes for each of the members of the group
7) Et al.

Such persons would be in violation of appropriate Federal and State statutes.

PROVISION OF LICENSING AGREEMENTS – Recognized educational, commercial, industrial, and governmental institutions and organizations, and others legitimately engaged in educational pursuits, including training, testing, and measurement activities, may address request for a licensing agreement to the copyright owners, who will determine whether, and under what conditions, including fees and charges, the materials in this book may be used them. In other words, a licensing facility exists for the legitimate use of the material in this book on other than an individual basis. However, it is asseverated and affirmed here that the material in this book CANNOT be used without the receipt of the express permission of such a licensing agreement from the Publishers. Inquiries re licensing should be addressed to the company, attention rights and permissions department.

All rights reserved, including the right of reproduction in whole or in part, in any form or by any means, electronic or mechanical, including photocopying, recording, or by any information storage and retrieval system, without permission in writing from the Publisher.

Copyright © 2024 by
National Learning Corporation

212 Michael Drive, Syosset, NY 11791
(516) 921-8888 • www.passbooks.com
E-mail: info@passbooks.com

PUBLISHED IN THE UNITED STATES OF AMERICA

PASSBOOK® SERIES

THE *PASSBOOK® SERIES* has been created to prepare applicants and candidates for the ultimate academic battlefield – the examination room.

At some time in our lives, each and every one of us may be required to take an examination – for validation, matriculation, admission, qualification, registration, certification, or licensure.

Based on the assumption that every applicant or candidate has met the basic formal educational standards, has taken the required number of courses, and read the necessary texts, the *PASSBOOK® SERIES* furnishes the one special preparation which may assure passing with confidence, instead of failing with insecurity. Examination questions – together with answers – are furnished as the basic vehicle for study so that the mysteries of the examination and its compounding difficulties may be eliminated or diminished by a sure method.

This book is meant to help you pass your examination provided that you qualify and are serious in your objective.

The entire field is reviewed through the huge store of content information which is succinctly presented through a provocative and challenging approach – the question-and-answer method.

A climate of success is established by furnishing the correct answers at the end of each test.

You soon learn to recognize types of questions, forms of questions, and patterns of questioning. You may even begin to anticipate expected outcomes.

You perceive that many questions are repeated or adapted so that you can gain acute insights, which may enable you to score many sure points.

You learn how to confront new questions, or types of questions, and to attack them confidently and work out the correct answers.

You note objectives and emphases, and recognize pitfalls and dangers, so that you may make positive educational adjustments.

Moreover, you are kept fully informed in relation to new concepts, methods, practices, and directions in the field.

You discover that you are actually taking the examination all the time: you are preparing for the examination by "taking" an examination, not by reading extraneous and/or supererogatory textbooks.

In short, this PASSBOOK®, used directedly, should be an important factor in helping you to pass your test.

ADMINISTRATIVE ANALYST

DUTIES
Conducts field audits and job evaluations; participates in feasibility studies and makes subsequent recommendations; participates in cost comparison studies and outlines methods by which recommendation can be effected; analyzes budget requests of departments and agencies including capital expenditures; analyzes proposals and prepares grant applications for federal or state funded programs maintains a comprehensive inventory of programs financed through federal and state grants; develops flow charts and tables of organization; and makes recommendations concerning the expanded use of data processing methods.

SCOPE OF THE WRITTEN TEST
The written test will cover knowledge, skills, and/or abilities in such areas as:
1. Administrative analysis;
2. Budgeting;
3. Understanding and interpreting written material;
4. Understanding and interpreting tabular material; and
5. Preparing written material.

HOW TO TAKE A TEST

I. YOU MUST PASS AN EXAMINATION

A. WHAT EVERY CANDIDATE SHOULD KNOW

Examination applicants often ask us for help in preparing for the written test. What can I study in advance? What kinds of questions will be asked? How will the test be given? How will the papers be graded?

As an applicant for a civil service examination, you may be wondering about some of these things. Our purpose here is to suggest effective methods of advance study and to describe civil service examinations.

Your chances for success on this examination can be increased if you know how to prepare. Those "pre-examination jitters" can be reduced if you know what to expect. You can even experience an adventure in good citizenship if you know why civil service exams are given.

B. WHY ARE CIVIL SERVICE EXAMINATIONS GIVEN?

Civil service examinations are important to you in two ways. As a citizen, you want public jobs filled by employees who know how to do their work. As a job seeker, you want a fair chance to compete for that job on an equal footing with other candidates. The best-known means of accomplishing this two-fold goal is the competitive examination.

Exams are widely publicized throughout the nation. They may be administered for jobs in federal, state, city, municipal, town or village governments or agencies.

Any citizen may apply, with some limitations, such as the age or residence of applicants. Your experience and education may be reviewed to see whether you meet the requirements for the particular examination. When these requirements exist, they are reasonable and applied consistently to all applicants. Thus, a competitive examination may cause you some uneasiness now, but it is your privilege and safeguard.

C. HOW ARE CIVIL SERVICE EXAMS DEVELOPED?

Examinations are carefully written by trained technicians who are specialists in the field known as "psychological measurement," in consultation with recognized authorities in the field of work that the test will cover. These experts recommend the subject matter areas or skills to be tested; only those knowledges or skills important to your success on the job are included. The most reliable books and source materials available are used as references. Together, the experts and technicians judge the difficulty level of the questions.

Test technicians know how to phrase questions so that the problem is clearly stated. Their ethics do not permit "trick" or "catch" questions. Questions may have been tried out on sample groups, or subjected to statistical analysis, to determine their usefulness.

Written tests are often used in combination with performance tests, ratings of training and experience, and oral interviews. All of these measures combine to form the best-known means of finding the right person for the right job.

II. HOW TO PASS THE WRITTEN TEST

A. NATURE OF THE EXAMINATION

To prepare intelligently for civil service examinations, you should know how they differ from school examinations you have taken. In school you were assigned certain definite pages to read or subjects to cover. The examination questions were quite detailed and usually emphasized memory. Civil service exams, on the other hand, try to discover your present ability to perform the duties of a position, plus your potentiality to learn these duties. In other words, a civil service exam attempts to predict how successful you will be. Questions cover such a broad area that they cannot be as minute and detailed as school exam questions.

In the public service similar kinds of work, or positions, are grouped together in one "class." This process is known as *position-classification*. All the positions in a class are paid according to the salary range for that class. One class title covers all of these positions, and they are all tested by the same examination.

B. FOUR BASIC STEPS

1) Study the announcement

How, then, can you know what subjects to study? Our best answer is: "Learn as much as possible about the class of positions for which you've applied." The exam will test the knowledge, skills and abilities needed to do the work.

Your most valuable source of information about the position you want is the official exam announcement. This announcement lists the training and experience qualifications. Check these standards and apply only if you come reasonably close to meeting them.

The brief description of the position in the examination announcement offers some clues to the subjects which will be tested. Think about the job itself. Review the duties in your mind. Can you perform them, or are there some in which you are rusty? Fill in the blank spots in your preparation.

Many jurisdictions preview the written test in the exam announcement by including a section called "Knowledge and Abilities Required," "Scope of the Examination," or some similar heading. Here you will find out specifically what fields will be tested.

2) Review your own background

Once you learn in general what the position is all about, and what you need to know to do the work, ask yourself which subjects you already know fairly well and which need improvement. You may wonder whether to concentrate on improving your strong areas or on building some background in your fields of weakness. When the announcement has specified "some knowledge" or "considerable knowledge," or has used adjectives like "beginning principles of…" or "advanced … methods," you can get a clue as to the number and difficulty of questions to be asked in any given field. More questions, and hence broader coverage, would be included for those subjects which are more important in the work. Now weigh your strengths and weaknesses against the job requirements and prepare accordingly.

3) Determine the level of the position

Another way to tell how intensively you should prepare is to understand the level of the job for which you are applying. Is it the entering level? In other words, is this the position in which beginners in a field of work are hired? Or is it an intermediate or advanced level? Sometimes this is indicated by such words as "Junior" or "Senior" in the class title. Other jurisdictions use Roman numerals to designate the level – Clerk I, Clerk II, for example. The word "Supervisor" sometimes appears in the title. If the level is not indicated by the title, check the description of duties. Will you be working under very close supervision, or will you have responsibility for independent decisions in this work?

4) Choose appropriate study materials

Now that you know the subjects to be examined and the relative amount of each subject to be covered, you can choose suitable study materials. For beginning level jobs, or even advanced ones, if you have a pronounced weakness in some aspect of your training, read a modern, standard textbook in that field. Be sure it is up to date and has general coverage. Such books are normally available at your library, and the librarian will be glad to help you locate one. For entry-level positions, questions of appropriate difficulty are chosen -- neither highly advanced questions, nor those too simple. Such questions require careful thought but not advanced training.

If the position for which you are applying is technical or advanced, you will read more advanced, specialized material. If you are already familiar with the basic principles of your field, elementary textbooks would waste your time. Concentrate on advanced textbooks and technical periodicals. Think through the concepts and review difficult problems in your field.

These are all general sources. You can get more ideas on your own initiative, following these leads. For example, training manuals and publications of the government agency which employs workers in your field can be useful, particularly for technical and professional positions. A letter or visit to the government department involved may result in more specific study suggestions, and certainly will provide you with a more definite idea of the exact nature of the position you are seeking.

III. KINDS OF TESTS

Tests are used for purposes other than measuring knowledge and ability to perform specified duties. For some positions, it is equally important to test ability to make adjustments to new situations or to profit from training. In others, basic mental abilities not dependent on information are essential. Questions which test these things may not appear as pertinent to the duties of the position as those which test for knowledge and information. Yet they are often highly important parts of a fair examination. For very general questions, it is almost impossible to help you direct your study efforts. What we can do is to point out some of the more common of these general abilities needed in public service positions and describe some typical questions.

1) General information

Broad, general information has been found useful for predicting job success in some kinds of work. This is tested in a variety of ways, from vocabulary lists to questions about current events. Basic background in some field of work, such as sociology or economics, may be sampled in a group of questions. Often these are principles which have become familiar to most persons through exposure rather than through formal training. It is difficult to advise you how to study for these questions; being alert to the world around you is our best suggestion.

2) Verbal ability

An example of an ability needed in many positions is verbal or language ability. Verbal ability is, in brief, the ability to use and understand words. Vocabulary and grammar tests are typical measures of this ability. Reading comprehension or paragraph interpretation questions are common in many kinds of civil service tests. You are given a paragraph of written material and asked to find its central meaning.

3) Numerical ability
Number skills can be tested by the familiar arithmetic problem, by checking paired lists of numbers to see which are alike and which are different, or by interpreting charts and graphs. In the latter test, a graph may be printed in the test booklet which you are asked to use as the basis for answering questions.

4) Observation
A popular test for law-enforcement positions is the observation test. A picture is shown to you for several minutes, then taken away. Questions about the picture test your ability to observe both details and larger elements.

5) Following directions
In many positions in the public service, the employee must be able to carry out written instructions dependably and accurately. You may be given a chart with several columns, each column listing a variety of information. The questions require you to carry out directions involving the information given in the chart.

6) Skills and aptitudes
Performance tests effectively measure some manual skills and aptitudes. When the skill is one in which you are trained, such as typing or shorthand, you can practice. These tests are often very much like those given in business school or high school courses. For many of the other skills and aptitudes, however, no short-time preparation can be made. Skills and abilities natural to you or that you have developed throughout your lifetime are being tested.

Many of the general questions just described provide all the data needed to answer the questions and ask you to use your reasoning ability to find the answers. Your best preparation for these tests, as well as for tests of facts and ideas, is to be at your physical and mental best. You, no doubt, have your own methods of getting into an exam-taking mood and keeping "in shape." The next section lists some ideas on this subject.

IV. KINDS OF QUESTIONS

Only rarely is the "essay" question, which you answer in narrative form, used in civil service tests. Civil service tests are usually of the short-answer type. Full instructions for answering these questions will be given to you at the examination. But in case this is your first experience with short-answer questions and separate answer sheets, here is what you need to know:

1) Multiple-choice Questions
Most popular of the short-answer questions is the "multiple choice" or "best answer" question. It can be used, for example, to test for factual knowledge, ability to solve problems or judgment in meeting situations found at work.
A multiple-choice question is normally one of three types—
- It can begin with an incomplete statement followed by several possible endings. You are to find the one ending which *best* completes the statement, although some of the others may not be entirely wrong.
- It can also be a complete statement in the form of a question which is answered by choosing one of the statements listed.

- It can be in the form of a problem – again you select the best answer.

Here is an example of a multiple-choice question with a discussion which should give you some clues as to the method for choosing the right answer:

When an employee has a complaint about his assignment, the action which will *best* help him overcome his difficulty is to
        A. discuss his difficulty with his coworkers
        B. take the problem to the head of the organization
        C. take the problem to the person who gave him the assignment
        D. say nothing to anyone about his complaint

In answering this question, you should study each of the choices to find which is best. Consider choice "A" – Certainly an employee may discuss his complaint with fellow employees, but no change or improvement can result, and the complaint remains unresolved. Choice "B" is a poor choice since the head of the organization probably does not know what assignment you have been given, and taking your problem to him is known as "going over the head" of the supervisor. The supervisor, or person who made the assignment, is the person who can clarify it or correct any injustice. Choice "C" is, therefore, correct. To say nothing, as in choice "D," is unwise. Supervisors have and interest in knowing the problems employees are facing, and the employee is seeking a solution to his problem.

2) True/False Questions

The "true/false" or "right/wrong" form of question is sometimes used. Here a complete statement is given. Your job is to decide whether the statement is right or wrong.

SAMPLE: A roaming cell-phone call to a nearby city costs less than a non-roaming call to a distant city.

This statement is wrong, or false, since roaming calls are more expensive.

This is not a complete list of all possible question forms, although most of the others are variations of these common types. You will always get complete directions for answering questions. Be sure you understand *how* to mark your answers – ask questions until you do.

V. RECORDING YOUR ANSWERS

Computer terminals are used more and more today for many different kinds of exams.

For an examination with very few applicants, you may be told to record your answers in the test booklet itself. Separate answer sheets are much more common. If this separate answer sheet is to be scored by machine – and this is often the case – it is highly important that you mark your answers correctly in order to get credit.

An electronic scoring machine is often used in civil service offices because of the speed with which papers can be scored. Machine-scored answer sheets must be marked with a pencil, which will be given to you. This pencil has a high graphite content which responds to the electronic scoring machine. As a matter of fact, stray dots may register as answers, so do not let your pencil rest on the answer sheet while you are pondering the correct answer. Also, if your pencil lead breaks or is otherwise defective, ask for another.

Since the answer sheet will be dropped in a slot in the scoring machine, be careful not to bend the corners or get the paper crumpled.

The answer sheet normally has five vertical columns of numbers, with 30 numbers to a column. These numbers correspond to the question numbers in your test booklet. After each number, going across the page are four or five pairs of dotted lines. These short dotted lines have small letters or numbers above them. The first two pairs may also have a "T" or "F" above the letters. This indicates that the first two pairs only are to be used if the questions are of the true-false type. If the questions are multiple choice, disregard the "T" and "F" and pay attention only to the small letters or numbers.

Answer your questions in the manner of the sample that follows:

32. The largest city in the United States is
    A. Washington, D.C.
    B. New York City
    C. Chicago
    D. Detroit
    E. San Francisco

1) Choose the answer you think is best. (New York City is the largest, so "B" is correct.)
2) Find the row of dotted lines numbered the same as the question you are answering. (Find row number 32)
3) Find the pair of dotted lines corresponding to the answer. (Find the pair of lines under the mark "B.")
4) Make a solid black mark between the dotted lines.

VI. BEFORE THE TEST

Common sense will help you find procedures to follow to get ready for an examination. Too many of us, however, overlook these sensible measures. Indeed, nervousness and fatigue have been found to be the most serious reasons why applicants fail to do their best on civil service tests. Here is a list of reminders:

- Begin your preparation early – Don't wait until the last minute to go scurrying around for books and materials or to find out what the position is all about.
- Prepare continuously – An hour a night for a week is better than an all-night cram session. This has been definitely established. What is more, a night a week for a month will return better dividends than crowding your study into a shorter period of time.
- Locate the place of the exam – You have been sent a notice telling you when and where to report for the examination. If the location is in a different town or otherwise unfamiliar to you, it would be well to inquire the best route and learn something about the building.
- Relax the night before the test – Allow your mind to rest. Do not study at all that night. Plan some mild recreation or diversion; then go to bed early and get a good night's sleep.
- Get up early enough to make a leisurely trip to the place for the test – This way unforeseen events, traffic snarls, unfamiliar buildings, etc. will not upset you.
- Dress comfortably – A written test is not a fashion show. You will be known by number and not by name, so wear something comfortable.

- Leave excess paraphernalia at home – Shopping bags and odd bundles will get in your way. You need bring only the items mentioned in the official notice you received; usually everything you need is provided. Do not bring reference books to the exam. They will only confuse those last minutes and be taken away from you when in the test room.
- Arrive somewhat ahead of time – If because of transportation schedules you must get there very early, bring a newspaper or magazine to take your mind off yourself while waiting.
- Locate the examination room – When you have found the proper room, you will be directed to the seat or part of the room where you will sit. Sometimes you are given a sheet of instructions to read while you are waiting. Do not fill out any forms until you are told to do so; just read them and be prepared.
- Relax and prepare to listen to the instructions
- If you have any physical problem that may keep you from doing your best, be sure to tell the test administrator. If you are sick or in poor health, you really cannot do your best on the exam. You can come back and take the test some other time.

VII. AT THE TEST

The day of the test is here and you have the test booklet in your hand. The temptation to get going is very strong. Caution! There is more to success than knowing the right answers. You must know how to identify your papers and understand variations in the type of short-answer question used in this particular examination. Follow these suggestions for maximum results from your efforts:

1) Cooperate with the monitor

The test administrator has a duty to create a situation in which you can be as much at ease as possible. He will give instructions, tell you when to begin, check to see that you are marking your answer sheet correctly, and so on. He is not there to guard you, although he will see that your competitors do not take unfair advantage. He wants to help you do your best.

2) Listen to all instructions

Don't jump the gun! Wait until you understand all directions. In most civil service tests you get more time than you need to answer the questions. So don't be in a hurry. Read each word of instructions until you clearly understand the meaning. Study the examples, listen to all announcements and follow directions. Ask questions if you do not understand what to do.

3) Identify your papers

Civil service exams are usually identified by number only. You will be assigned a number; you must not put your name on your test papers. Be sure to copy your number correctly. Since more than one exam may be given, copy your exact examination title.

4) Plan your time

Unless you are told that a test is a "speed" or "rate of work" test, speed itself is usually not important. Time enough to answer all the questions will be provided, but this does not mean that you have all day. An overall time limit has been set. Divide the total time (in minutes) by the number of questions to determine the approximate time you have for each question.

5) Do not linger over difficult questions

If you come across a difficult question, mark it with a paper clip (useful to have along) and come back to it when you have been through the booklet. One caution if you do this – be sure to skip a number on your answer sheet as well. Check often to be sure that you have not lost your place and that you are marking in the row numbered the same as the question you are answering.

6) Read the questions

Be sure you know what the question asks! Many capable people are unsuccessful because they failed to *read* the questions correctly.

7) Answer all questions

Unless you have been instructed that a penalty will be deducted for incorrect answers, it is better to guess than to omit a question.

8) Speed tests

It is often better NOT to guess on speed tests. It has been found that on timed tests people are tempted to spend the last few seconds before time is called in marking answers at random – without even reading them – in the hope of picking up a few extra points. To discourage this practice, the instructions may warn you that your score will be "corrected" for guessing. That is, a penalty will be applied. The incorrect answers will be deducted from the correct ones, or some other penalty formula will be used.

9) Review your answers

If you finish before time is called, go back to the questions you guessed or omitted to give them further thought. Review other answers if you have time.

10) Return your test materials

If you are ready to leave before others have finished or time is called, take ALL your materials to the monitor and leave quietly. Never take any test material with you. The monitor can discover whose papers are not complete, and taking a test booklet may be grounds for disqualification.

VIII. EXAMINATION TECHNIQUES

1) Read the general instructions carefully. These are usually printed on the first page of the exam booklet. As a rule, these instructions refer to the timing of the examination; the fact that you should not start work until the signal and must stop work at a signal, etc. If there are any *special* instructions, such as a choice of questions to be answered, make sure that you note this instruction carefully.

2) When you are ready to start work on the examination, that is as soon as the signal has been given, read the instructions to each question booklet, underline any key words or phrases, such as *least, best, outline, describe* and the like. In this way you will tend to answer as requested rather than discover on reviewing your paper that you *listed without describing*, that you selected the *worst* choice rather than the *best* choice, etc.

3) If the examination is of the objective or multiple-choice type – that is, each question will also give a series of possible answers: A, B, C or D, and you are called upon to select the best answer and write the letter next to that answer on your answer paper – it is advisable to start answering each question in turn. There may be anywhere from 50 to 100 such questions in the three or four hours allotted and you can see how much time would be taken if you read through all the questions before beginning to answer any. Furthermore, if you come across a question or group of questions which you know would be difficult to answer, it would undoubtedly affect your handling of all the other questions.

4) If the examination is of the essay type and contains but a few questions, it is a moot point as to whether you should read all the questions before starting to answer any one. Of course, if you are given a choice – say five out of seven and the like – then it is essential to read all the questions so you can eliminate the two that are most difficult. If, however, you are asked to answer all the questions, there may be danger in trying to answer the easiest one first because you may find that you will spend too much time on it. The best technique is to answer the first question, then proceed to the second, etc.

5) Time your answers. Before the exam begins, write down the time it started, then add the time allowed for the examination and write down the time it must be completed, then divide the time available somewhat as follows:
    - If 3-1/2 hours are allowed, that would be 210 minutes. If you have 80 objective-type questions, that would be an average of 2-1/2 minutes per question. Allow yourself no more than 2 minutes per question, or a total of 160 minutes, which will permit about 50 minutes to review.
    - If for the time allotment of 210 minutes there are 7 essay questions to answer, that would average about 30 minutes a question. Give yourself only 25 minutes per question so that you have about 35 minutes to review.

6) The most important instruction is to *read each question* and make sure you know what is wanted. The second most important instruction is to *time yourself properly* so that you answer every question. The third most important instruction is to *answer every question*. Guess if you have to but include something for each question. Remember that you will receive no credit for a blank and will probably receive some credit if you write something in answer to an essay question. If you guess a letter – say "B" for a multiple-choice question – you may have guessed right. If you leave a blank as an answer to a multiple-choice question, the examiners may respect your feelings but it will not add a point to your score. Some exams may penalize you for wrong answers, so in such cases *only*, you may not want to guess unless you have some basis for your answer.

7) Suggestions
    a. Objective-type questions
        1. Examine the question booklet for proper sequence of pages and questions
        2. Read all instructions carefully
        3. Skip any question which seems too difficult; return to it after all other questions have been answered
        4. Apportion your time properly; do not spend too much time on any single question or group of questions

5. Note and underline key words – *all, most, fewest, least, best, worst, same, opposite,* etc.
6. Pay particular attention to negatives
7. Note unusual option, e.g., unduly long, short, complex, different or similar in content to the body of the question
8. Observe the use of "hedging" words – *probably, may, most likely,* etc.
9. Make sure that your answer is put next to the same number as the question
10. Do not second-guess unless you have good reason to believe the second answer is definitely more correct
11. Cross out original answer if you decide another answer is more accurate; do not erase until you are ready to hand your paper in
12. Answer all questions; guess unless instructed otherwise
13. Leave time for review

  b. Essay questions
    1. Read each question carefully
    2. Determine exactly what is wanted. Underline key words or phrases.
    3. Decide on outline or paragraph answer
    4. Include many different points and elements unless asked to develop any one or two points or elements
    5. Show impartiality by giving pros and cons unless directed to select one side only
    6. Make and write down any assumptions you find necessary to answer the questions
    7. Watch your English, grammar, punctuation and choice of words
    8. Time your answers; don't crowd material

8) Answering the essay question

Most essay questions can be answered by framing the specific response around several key words or ideas. Here are a few such key words or ideas:

M's: manpower, materials, methods, money, management
P's: purpose, program, policy, plan, procedure, practice, problems, pitfalls, personnel, public relations

  a. Six basic steps in handling problems:
    1. Preliminary plan and background development
    2. Collect information, data and facts
    3. Analyze and interpret information, data and facts
    4. Analyze and develop solutions as well as make recommendations
    5. Prepare report and sell recommendations
    6. Install recommendations and follow up effectiveness

  b. Pitfalls to avoid
    1. *Taking things for granted* – A statement of the situation does not necessarily imply that each of the elements is necessarily true; for example, a complaint may be invalid and biased so that all that can be taken for granted is that a complaint has been registered

2. *Considering only one side of a situation* – Wherever possible, indicate several alternatives and then point out the reasons you selected the best one
3. *Failing to indicate follow up* – Whenever your answer indicates action on your part, make certain that you will take proper follow-up action to see how successful your recommendations, procedures or actions turn out to be
4. *Taking too long in answering any single question* – Remember to time your answers properly

IX. AFTER THE TEST

Scoring procedures differ in detail among civil service jurisdictions although the general principles are the same. Whether the papers are hand-scored or graded by machine we have described, they are nearly always graded by number. That is, the person who marks the paper knows only the number – never the name – of the applicant. Not until all the papers have been graded will they be matched with names. If other tests, such as training and experience or oral interview ratings have been given, scores will be combined. Different parts of the examination usually have different weights. For example, the written test might count 60 percent of the final grade, and a rating of training and experience 40 percent. In many jurisdictions, veterans will have a certain number of points added to their grades.

After the final grade has been determined, the names are placed in grade order and an eligible list is established. There are various methods for resolving ties between those who get the same final grade – probably the most common is to place first the name of the person whose application was received first. Job offers are made from the eligible list in the order the names appear on it. You will be notified of your grade and your rank as soon as all these computations have been made. This will be done as rapidly as possible.

People who are found to meet the requirements in the announcement are called "eligibles." Their names are put on a list of eligible candidates. An eligible's chances of getting a job depend on how high he stands on this list and how fast agencies are filling jobs from the list.

When a job is to be filled from a list of eligibles, the agency asks for the names of people on the list of eligibles for that job. When the civil service commission receives this request, it sends to the agency the names of the three people highest on this list. Or, if the job to be filled has specialized requirements, the office sends the agency the names of the top three persons who meet these requirements from the general list.

The appointing officer makes a choice from among the three people whose names were sent to him. If the selected person accepts the appointment, the names of the others are put back on the list to be considered for future openings.

That is the rule in hiring from all kinds of eligible lists, whether they are for typist, carpenter, chemist, or something else. For every vacancy, the appointing officer has his choice of any one of the top three eligibles on the list. This explains why the person whose name is on top of the list sometimes does not get an appointment when some of the persons lower on the list do. If the appointing officer chooses the second or third eligible, the No. 1 eligible does not get a job at once, but stays on the list until he is appointed or the list is terminated.

X. HOW TO PASS THE INTERVIEW TEST

The examination for which you applied requires an oral interview test. You have already taken the written test and you are now being called for the interview test – the final part of the formal examination.

You may think that it is not possible to prepare for an interview test and that there are no procedures to follow during an interview. Our purpose is to point out some things you can do in advance that will help you and some good rules to follow and pitfalls to avoid while you are being interviewed.

What is an interview supposed to test?

The written examination is designed to test the technical knowledge and competence of the candidate; the oral is designed to evaluate intangible qualities, not readily measured otherwise, and to establish a list showing the relative fitness of each candidate – as measured against his competitors – for the position sought. Scoring is not on the basis of "right" and "wrong," but on a sliding scale of values ranging from "not passable" to "outstanding." As a matter of fact, it is possible to achieve a relatively low score without a single "incorrect" answer because of evident weakness in the qualities being measured.

Occasionally, an examination may consist entirely of an oral test – either an individual or a group oral. In such cases, information is sought concerning the technical knowledges and abilities of the candidate, since there has been no written examination for this purpose. More commonly, however, an oral test is used to supplement a written examination.

Who conducts interviews?

The composition of oral boards varies among different jurisdictions. In nearly all, a representative of the personnel department serves as chairman. One of the members of the board may be a representative of the department in which the candidate would work. In some cases, "outside experts" are used, and, frequently, a businessman or some other representative of the general public is asked to serve. Labor and management or other special groups may be represented. The aim is to secure the services of experts in the appropriate field.

However the board is composed, it is a good idea (and not at all improper or unethical) to ascertain in advance of the interview who the members are and what groups they represent. When you are introduced to them, you will have some idea of their backgrounds and interests, and at least you will not stutter and stammer over their names.

What should be done before the interview?

While knowledge about the board members is useful and takes some of the surprise element out of the interview, there is other preparation which is more substantive. It *is* possible to prepare for an oral interview – in several ways:

1) Keep a copy of your application and review it carefully before the interview

This may be the only document before the oral board, and the starting point of the interview. Know what education and experience you have listed there, and the sequence and dates of all of it. Sometimes the board will ask you to review the highlights of your experience for them; you should not have to hem and haw doing it.

2) Study the class specification and the examination announcement

Usually, the oral board has one or both of these to guide them. The qualities, characteristics or knowledges required by the position sought are stated in these documents. They offer valuable clues as to the nature of the oral interview. For example, if the job involves supervisory responsibilities, the announcement will usually indicate that knowledge of modern supervisory methods and the qualifications of the candidate as a supervisor will be tested. If so, you can expect such questions, frequently in the form of a hypothetical situation which you are expected to solve. NEVER go into an oral without knowledge of the duties and responsibilities of the job you seek.

3) Think through each qualification required

Try to visualize the kind of questions you would ask if you were a board member. How well could you answer them? Try especially to appraise your own knowledge and background in each area, *measured against the job sought*, and identify any areas in which you are weak. Be critical and realistic – do not flatter yourself.

4) Do some general reading in areas in which you feel you may be weak

For example, if the job involves supervision and your past experience has NOT, some general reading in supervisory methods and practices, particularly in the field of human relations, might be useful. Do NOT study agency procedures or detailed manuals. The oral board will be testing your understanding and capacity, not your memory.

5) Get a good night's sleep and watch your general health and mental attitude

You will want a clear head at the interview. Take care of a cold or any other minor ailment, and of course, no hangovers.

What should be done on the day of the interview?

Now comes the day of the interview itself. Give yourself plenty of time to get there. Plan to arrive somewhat ahead of the scheduled time, particularly if your appointment is in the fore part of the day. If a previous candidate fails to appear, the board might be ready for you a bit early. By early afternoon an oral board is almost invariably behind schedule if there are many candidates, and you may have to wait. Take along a book or magazine to read, or your application to review, but leave any extraneous material in the waiting room when you go in for your interview. In any event, relax and compose yourself.

The matter of dress is important. The board is forming impressions about you – from your experience, your manners, your attitude, and your appearance. Give your personal appearance careful attention. Dress your best, but not your flashiest. Choose conservative, appropriate clothing, and be sure it is immaculate. This is a business interview, and your appearance should indicate that you regard it as such. Besides, being well groomed and properly dressed will help boost your confidence.

Sooner or later, someone will call your name and escort you into the interview room. *This is it.* From here on you are on your own. It is too late for any more preparation. But remember, you asked for this opportunity to prove your fitness, and you are here because your request was granted.

What happens when you go in?

The usual sequence of events will be as follows: The clerk (who is often the board stenographer) will introduce you to the chairman of the oral board, who will introduce you to the other members of the board. Acknowledge the introductions before you sit down. Do not be surprised if you find a microphone facing you or a stenotypist sitting by. Oral interviews are usually recorded in the event of an appeal or other review.

Usually the chairman of the board will open the interview by reviewing the highlights of your education and work experience from your application – primarily for the benefit of the other members of the board, as well as to get the material into the record. Do not interrupt or comment unless there is an error or significant misinterpretation; if that is the case, do not hesitate. But do not quibble about insignificant matters. Also, he will usually ask you some question about your education, experience or your present job – partly to get you to start talking and to establish the interviewing "rapport." He may start the actual questioning, or turn it over to one of the other members. Frequently, each member undertakes the questioning on a particular area, one in which he is perhaps most competent, so you can expect each member to participate in the examination. Because time is limited, you may also expect some rather abrupt switches in the direction the questioning takes, so do not be upset by it. Normally, a board member will not pursue a single line of questioning unless he discovers a particular strength or weakness.

After each member has participated, the chairman will usually ask whether any member has any further questions, then will ask you if you have anything you wish to add. Unless you are expecting this question, it may floor you. Worse, it may start you off on an extended, extemporaneous speech. The board is not usually seeking more information. The question is principally to offer you a last opportunity to present further qualifications or to indicate that you have nothing to add. So, if you feel that a significant qualification or characteristic has been overlooked, it is proper to point it out in a sentence or so. Do not compliment the board on the thoroughness of their examination – they have been sketchy, and you know it. If you wish, merely say, "No thank you, I have nothing further to add." This is a point where you can "talk yourself out" of a good impression or fail to present an important bit of information. Remember, *you close the interview yourself.*

The chairman will then say, "That is all, Mr. _____, thank you." Do not be startled; the interview is over, and quicker than you think. Thank him, gather your belongings and take your leave. Save your sigh of relief for the other side of the door.

How to put your best foot forward

Throughout this entire process, you may feel that the board individually and collectively is trying to pierce your defenses, seek out your hidden weaknesses and embarrass and confuse you. Actually, this is not true. They are obliged to make an appraisal of your qualifications for the job you are seeking, and they want to see you in your best light. Remember, they must interview all candidates and a non-cooperative candidate may become a failure in spite of their best efforts to bring out his qualifications. Here are 15 suggestions that will help you:

1) Be natural – Keep your attitude confident, not cocky

If you are not confident that you can do the job, do not expect the board to be. Do not apologize for your weaknesses, try to bring out your strong points. The board is interested in a positive, not negative, presentation. Cockiness will antagonize any board member and make him wonder if you are covering up a weakness by a false show of strength.

2) Get comfortable, but don't lounge or sprawl

Sit erectly but not stiffly. A careless posture may lead the board to conclude that you are careless in other things, or at least that you are not impressed by the importance of the occasion. Either conclusion is natural, even if incorrect. Do not fuss with your clothing, a pencil or an ashtray. Your hands may occasionally be useful to emphasize a point; do not let them become a point of distraction.

3) Do not wisecrack or make small talk

This is a serious situation, and your attitude should show that you consider it as such. Further, the time of the board is limited – they do not want to waste it, and neither should you.

4) Do not exaggerate your experience or abilities
In the first place, from information in the application or other interviews and sources, the board may know more about you than you think. Secondly, you probably will not get away with it. An experienced board is rather adept at spotting such a situation, so do not take the chance.

5) If you know a board member, do not make a point of it, yet do not hide it
Certainly you are not fooling him, and probably not the other members of the board. Do not try to take advantage of your acquaintanceship – it will probably do you little good.

6) Do not dominate the interview
Let the board do that. They will give you the clues – do not assume that you have to do all the talking. Realize that the board has a number of questions to ask you, and do not try to take up all the interview time by showing off your extensive knowledge of the answer to the first one.

7) Be attentive
You only have 20 minutes or so, and you should keep your attention at its sharpest throughout. When a member is addressing a problem or question to you, give him your undivided attention. Address your reply principally to him, but do not exclude the other board members.

8) Do not interrupt
A board member may be stating a problem for you to analyze. He will ask you a question when the time comes. Let him state the problem, and wait for the question.

9) Make sure you understand the question
Do not try to answer until you are sure what the question is. If it is not clear, restate it in your own words or ask the board member to clarify it for you. However, do not haggle about minor elements.

10) Reply promptly but not hastily
A common entry on oral board rating sheets is "candidate responded readily," or "candidate hesitated in replies." Respond as promptly and quickly as you can, but do not jump to a hasty, ill-considered answer.

11) Do not be peremptory in your answers
A brief answer is proper – but do not fire your answer back. That is a losing game from your point of view. The board member can probably ask questions much faster than you can answer them.

12) Do not try to create the answer you think the board member wants
He is interested in what kind of mind you have and how it works – not in playing games. Furthermore, he can usually spot this practice and will actually grade you down on it.

13) Do not switch sides in your reply merely to agree with a board member
Frequently, a member will take a contrary position merely to draw you out and to see if you are willing and able to defend your point of view. Do not start a debate, yet do not surrender a good position. If a position is worth taking, it is worth defending.

14) Do not be afraid to admit an error in judgment if you are shown to be wrong

The board knows that you are forced to reply without any opportunity for careful consideration. Your answer may be demonstrably wrong. If so, admit it and get on with the interview.

15) Do not dwell at length on your present job

The opening question may relate to your present assignment. Answer the question but do not go into an extended discussion. You are being examined for a *new* job, not your present one. As a matter of fact, try to phrase ALL your answers in terms of the job for which you are being examined.

Basis of Rating

Probably you will forget most of these "do's" and "don'ts" when you walk into the oral interview room. Even remembering them all will not ensure you a passing grade. Perhaps you did not have the qualifications in the first place. But remembering them will help you to put your best foot forward, without treading on the toes of the board members.

Rumor and popular opinion to the contrary notwithstanding, an oral board wants you to make the best appearance possible. They know you are under pressure – but they also want to see how you respond to it as a guide to what your reaction would be under the pressures of the job you seek. They will be influenced by the degree of poise you display, the personal traits you show and the manner in which you respond.

ABOUT THIS BOOK

This book contains tests divided into Examination Sections. Go through each test, answering every question in the margin. We have also attached a sample answer sheet at the back of the book that can be removed and used. At the end of each test look at the answer key and check your answers. On the ones you got wrong, look at the right answer choice and learn. Do not fill in the answers first. Do not memorize the questions and answers, but understand the answer and principles involved. On your test, the questions will likely be different from the samples. Questions are changed and new ones added. If you understand these past questions you should have success with any changes that arise. Tests may consist of several types of questions. We have additional books on each subject should more study be advisable or necessary for you. Finally, the more you study, the better prepared you will be. This book is intended to be the last thing you study before you walk into the examination room. Prior study of relevant texts is also recommended. NLC publishes some of these in our Fundamental Series. Knowledge and good sense are important factors in passing your exam. Good luck also helps. So now study this Passbook, absorb the material contained within and take that knowledge into the examination. Then do your best to pass that exam.

EXAMINATION SECTION

EXAMINATION SECTION
TEST 1

DIRECTIONS: Each question or incomplete statement is followed by several suggested answers or completions. Select the one that BEST answers the question or completes the statement. *PRINT THE LETTER OF THE CORRECT ANSWER IN THE SPACE AT THE RIGHT.*

1. Of the following factors, which one is LEAST important in determining the size of staff needed in conducting an organization survey?
   The

   A. effectiveness of the personnel in supplying data for the study
   B. extent of report writing anticipated
   C. number of field locations and headquarters staff units to be covered
   D. number of individuals to be interviewed as part of fact finding

2. In planning a systems survey, which one of the following is MOST important in carrying out an effective survey after the purpose and scope of the survey has been determined? The

   A. format of the survey report
   B. methods and techniques to be employed
   C. personality problems which may materialize
   D. exact starting and completion dates

3. Which of the following is the BEST way of organizing a final report?

   A. Begin and end the report with a summary of conclusions showing how conclusions were changed as a result of findings and recommendations
   B. Begin the report with an overall summary and then place findings and recommendations in several sections
   C. Intertwine findings and conclusions in such a manner as to make the report readable and interesting
   D. Place the findings and recommendations in separate sections avoiding conclusions to the maximum extent possible

4. Which of the following disadvantages is the MOST serious in making reports verbally rather than in writing?

   A. An effective analyst may not be a good public speaker.
   B. Verbal reports are conveniently forgotten.
   C. It may not generate actions and follow-through by recipients.
   D. There is a lack of permanent record to which one may later refer.

5. Following a management survey, which of the following represents the MOST serious pitfall which may be made in recommending improvements?

   A. Failure to convince people of the benefits to be derived from the recommendations
   B. Failure to freely discuss recommendations with those who must live with them
   C. Tendency of the survey team to put their own personalities into the report
   D. Tendency to deal in personalities instead of dealing with objectives and sound management practices

6. A working outline for management analysts should include all of the following EXCEPT

   A. a chronological outline of the work steps
   B. a determination of background information needed
   C. the distribution of outline to key staff and line personnel
   D. preliminary conclusions

7. Which one of the following areas is the MOST critical for an analyst during the fact-finding stage of a study?

   A. Accuracy of data appearing in reports
   B. Attitude of those being interviewed by the analyst
   C. Observations and tentative conclusions reached by the analyst
   D. Suggestions and recommendations of interviewees

8. Creating an organization embraces all of the following areas of management EXCEPT

   A. clarification of objectives
   B. determining the number of people required to man the organization
   C. establishing operating budgets to make the plan effective
   D. proper structuring of all key positions

9. In an organization, the MAJOR barrier to accepting change is the

   A. assumption by management that everyone will willingly accept change
   B. failure by management to present proposed changes in a proper fashion
   C. lack of adaptive abilities on the part of employees
   D. lack of understanding on the part of employees of sound management principles

10. A supervisor who wishes to attain established objectives should concentrate on

    A. determining whether management is operating at maximum effectiveness
    B. making suggestions for improving the organization
    C. planning work assignments
    D. securing salary increases for needy employees

11. A usually competent employee complains that he does not understand the procedures to be followed in performing a certain task although the supervisor has explained them twice and has demonstrated them.
    Of the following, the BEST course of action for the supervisor to take is to

    A. ask the employee whether he has any problems which are bothering him
    B. assign someone else to the job
    C. explain the procedures again and demonstrate at the same time
    D. have the employee perform the job while he watches and gives additional instructions

12. GENERALLY, in order to be completely qualified as a supervisor, a person

    A. should be able to perform exceptionally well at least one of the jobs he supervises and have some knowledge of the others
    B. must have an intimate working knowledge of all facets of the jobs which he supervises
    C. should know the basic principles and procedures of the jobs he supervises
    D. need know little or nothing of the jobs which he supervises as long as he knows the principles of supervision

13. Which of the following contributes MOST to the problem of waste and inefficiency in offices?

    A. Cost control is a budget function primarily.
    B. Most organizations do not have soundly conceived budgets.
    C. Procedures improvement staffs have not as yet gained acceptance among white-collar workers.
    D. Supervisors generally are uninterested in making improvements.

14. Which of the following contributes MOST to the great number of duplicate reports and double-checking procedures frequently found in offices?
    The

    A. desire for protection
    B. desire to improve problem solving
    C. intent to *manage by exception*
    D. need for budget data

15. Which one of the following BEST identifies the narrow technician as compared with the broad-gauged analyst?
    He

    A. analyzes the activities of an agency
    B. attempts to form sound relationships with departmental personnel
    C. focuses attention on forms design and appearance
    D. follows work flow from one bureau to another by charting operational steps

16. The percentage of budget funds allocated to fixed overhead costs can be MOST effectively reduced by

    A. a soundly conceived *promotion from within* policy
    B. increasing the amount of work performed
    C. relocating to areas closer to the center of cities
    D. tightening the *fixed cost* portion of the budget

17. The term *span of control* USUALLY refers to

    A. individuals reporting to a common supervisor
    B. individuals with whom one individual has contact in the course of performing his assigned duties
    C. levels of supervision in an organization
    D. percentage of time in an organization devoted to supervisory duties

18. For an analyst, which of the following is generally LEAST important in conducting a management survey?

    A. Ability of employees to understand goals of the survey
    B. Attitude of supervisors of employees
    C. Availability of employees for interviews
    D. Cooperation of employees

19. Of the following, morale in an agency is generally MOST significantly affected by

    A. agency policies and procedures
    B. agency recognition of executives supporting agency goals
    C. the extent to which an agency meets its announced goals
    D. the number of management surveys conducted in an agency

20. Which of the following BEST describes the principle of *management by exception?*

    A. Allocating executive time and effort in direct relation to the dollar values of the budget
    B. Decentralizing management and dealing primarily with problem areas
    C. Measuring only direct costs
    D. Setting goals and objectives and managing only these

21. A WEAKNESS of many budgetary systems today is that they

    A. are subjectively determined by those most directly involved
    B. focus on management weakness rather than management strength
    C. only show variable costs
    D. show in detail why losses are occurring

22. Standards on which budgets are developed should be based PRIMARILY on

    A. a general consensus   B. agency wishes
    C. analytical studies   D. historical performance

23. The income, cost, and expense goals making up a budget are aimed at achieving a pre-determined objective but do not necessarily measure the lowest possible costs. This is PRIMARILY so because

    A. budget committees are accounting-oriented and are not sympathetic with the supervisor's personnel problems
    B. budget committees fail to recognize the difference between direct and indirect costs
    C. the level of expenditures provided for in a budget by budget committees is frequently an arbitrary rather than a scientifically determined amount
    D. budget committees spend considerable time evaluating data to the point that the material gathered is not representative or current

24. Linear programming has all of the following characteristics EXCEPT: It
    A. is concerned with an optimum position in relation to some objective
    B. involves the selection among alternatives or the appropriate combination of alternatives
    C. not only requires that variables be qualitative but also rests on the assumption that the relations among the variables are minimized
    D. takes into account constraints or limits within which the decision is to be reached

25. In the PERT planning system, the time in which a non-critical task can slip schedule without holding up a project is USUALLY called
    A. constraint
    B. duration time
    C. dead time
    D. float or slack

26. The Produc-trol board and Schedugraphs are commercial variations of the _____ chart.
    A. flow
    B. Gantt
    C. layout
    D. multiple activity

27. The item which cannot be analyzed by such schematic techniques as the frequency polygon and the histogram is the
    A. age of accounts receivable
    B. morale and cohesiveness of work groups
    C. number of accidents in a plant
    D. wage pattern

28. An essential employee benefit of work measurement which FREQUENTLY is the key to the successful implementation of such a program is
    A. equitable work distribution
    B. facilitation of the development of budgets
    C. measurement and control of office productivity
    D. prevention of unfair work distribution

29. An organizational arrangement whereby different employees perform different work steps upon the same work items at the same time is called the _____ method.
    A. functional
    B. homogenous
    C. parallel or linear arrangement
    D. unit assembly

30. Frequently, opposition to a management survey stems from an executive's feeling that he might be considered responsible for the unsatisfactory conditions that the project is aimed at correcting.
    To overcome this type of opposition, the analyst should GENERALLY
    A. avoid the issue altogether
    B. face the situation *head on* and, if the executive is responsible, tell him so
    C. offer a reasonable explanation for those conditions early enough in the discussion to forestall any implication of criticism
    D. place the blame for the unsatisfactory conditions at the lowest level in the organization to avoid incriminating the boss

31. Which of the following situations is LEAST likely to require a management survey?

    A. Changes in policy
    B. Management requests for additional manpower
    C. Legislation mandating changes in operating procedures
    D. Significantly lower costs than anticipated

32. The efficiency of a procedure is often influenced by the practices or performance of departments that play no direct part in carrying it out.
    In view of this, the analyst must

    A. disregard the practices or performance of departments that play no direct part in the procedure
    B. do the very best job within the department studied to compensate for the outside problems
    C. ask for assistance in solving the problems created by this situation
    D. study and evaluate the external factors to the extent that they bear on the problem

33. Which one of the following is NOT a key step in staff delegation and development?

    A. Evaluation of the completed job
    B. Preparation of a subordinate to accept additional duties
    C. Review of daily progress
    D. Selection of a suitable job to be delegated

34. Which one of the following is NOT an essential characteristic of effective delegation?

    A. In delegating, the supervisor is no longer responsible.
    B. The individual to whom authority is delegated must be accountable for fulfillment of the task.
    C. The individual to whom authority is delegated must clearly understand this authority
    D. The individual to whom authority is delegated must get honest recognition for a job well done.

35. Whenever a manager must determine how long an operation should take, he is involved with the problem of setting a time standard.
    To PROPERLY set time standards, the manager must distinguish between

    A. estimation processes and evaluation processes
    B. performance of the slowest employee and performance of the fastest employee
    C. stop watch study and work sampling
    D. synthetic and arbitrary systems

36. Assuming a report is needed, which approach USUALLY facilitates implementation?
    A

    A. draft report submitted to key people for review, discussion, modification, and then resubmission in final form
    B. report in final form which sets forth alternate recommended solutions
    C. report which sets forth the problems and the recommended solution in conformance with the desires of those most directly involved
    D. visual presentation with minimal report writing

37. Of the following elements, which is the LEAST important in writing a survey report?
    A

    A. definite course of action to be followed
    B. listing of benefits to be gained through implementation
    C. review of opinions as differentiated from facts
    D. summary of conclusions

38. Physical appearance and accuracy are important features in gaining acceptance to recommendations. Which one of the following might be OVERLOOKED in preparing a report which is to have wide distribution?

    A. A comprehensive index
    B. An attractive binder
    C. Proper spacing and page layout
    D. Charts and tables

39. The elimination of meaningless reports, although reducing the total information output, IMPROVES the management process by

    A. determining the number of employees required to perform the work assigned
    B. identifying the difference between direct and indirect costs
    C. increasing the effectiveness of executives
    D. limiting the budget to variable costs

40. In determining whether or not to use a computerized system as opposed to a manual system, which of the following would normally have the MOST influence on the decision?
    The

    A. availability of analysts and programmers to design and install the system
    B. availability of computer time
    C. basic premise that all computerized systems are superior to manual systems
    D. volume and complexity of transactions required

KEY (CORRECT ANSWERS)

1. A	11. D	21. A	31. D
2. B	12. C	22. C	32. D
3. B	13. C	23. C	33. C
4. D	14. A	24. C	34. A
5. D	15. C	25. D	35. A
6. D	16. B	26. B	36. A
7. C	17. A	27. B	37. C
8. C	18. A	28. A	38. B
9. B	19. A	29. D	39. C
10. C	20. B	30. C	40. D

TEST 2

DIRECTIONS: Each question or incomplete statement is followed by several suggested answers or completions. Select the one that BEST answers the question or completes the statement. *PRINT THE LETTER OF THE CORRECT ANSWER IN THE SPACE AT THE RIGHT*

1. The one of the following that is NOT normally involved in the development of a management information system is

    A. determination of the best method of preparing and presenting the required information
    B. determination of line and staff relationships within the various units of the organizational structure
    C. determination of what specific information is needed for decision-making and control
    D. identification of the critical aspects of the business, i.e., the end results and other elements of performance which need to be planned and controlled

2. The long-term growth in size and complexity of both business and government has increased management's dependence on more formal written summaries of operating results in place of the informal, on-the-spot observations and judgments of smaller organizations.
   In addition, there is a growing management need to

    A. increase the complexity of those phases of the management process which have previously been simplified
    B. increase the speed and accuracy of artificial intelligence
    C. measure the effectiveness of managerial performance
    D. reduce alcoholism by greatly limiting personal contacts between the various levels of management within the organization

3. Of the following, it is MOST essential that a management information system provide information needed for

    A. determining computer time requirements
    B. developing new office layouts
    C. drawing new organization charts
    D. planning and measuring results

4. The PRIMARY purpose of control reports is to

    A. compare actual performance with planned results
    B. determine staffing requirements
    C. determine the work flow
    D. develop a new budget

5. Which one of the following has the GREATEST negative impact on communications in a large organization?

    A. Delays in formulating variable policies relating to communications
    B. Failure to conduct comprehensive courses in communications skills
    C. Failure to get information to those who need it
    D. Unclear organizational objectives

6. Efficiency of an organization is significantly impacted by all of the following EXCEPT

    A. network connectivity
    B. software compatibility
    C. hardware upgrades
    D. cloud data storage

7. The type of computer configuration in which the data are processed at one time after they have been made a matter of record is known as

    A. batching   B. in line   C. off line   D. real time

8. A computer configuration system in which the input or output equipment is directly connected and operates under control of the computer is known as

    A. off line
    B. on line
    C. random access
    D. real time

9. A manager who wants to quickly analyze the output of a particular department would most likely refer to which one of the following?

    A. An Excel spreadsheet with production data logged by department
    B. Email reports submitted by department leaders
    C. Quarterly reports describing production targets and measurements
    D. An Excel spreadsheet with employee-generated survey data related to typical daily output and capabilities

10. Computers are generally considered to consist of four major sections. The one of the following which is NOT a major section is

    A. buffer
    B. control
    C. processing
    D. storage

11. Of the following, administrative control is PRIMARILY dependent upon

    A. adequate information
    B. a widespread spy network
    C. strict supervisors
    D. strong sanctions

12. Meticulous care must be exercised in writing the methodology section of the research report so that

    A. another investigator will achieve the same results if he repeats the study
    B. the interpretation of the findings cannot be challenged
    C. the report will be well balanced
    D. the rules of scientific logic are clearly indicated

13. When data are grouped into a frequency distribution, the *true mode* by definition is the _____ in the distribution.

    A. 50% point
    B. largest single range
    C. point of greatest concentration
    D. smallest single range

14. Which of the following is LEAST likely to be a potential benefit arising from the use of electronic data processing systems?

    A. Analysis of more data and analysis of data in greater depth than manual systems
    B. Increased speed and accuracy in information processing
    C. Lower capital expenditures for office equipment
    D. Reduced personnel costs in tabulating and reporting functions

15. A *grapevine* is BEST defined as

    A. a harmful method of communication
    B. a system of communication operative below the executive level
    C. an informal communication system of no functional importance to an organization
    D. the internal and non-systematic channel of communication within an organization

16. Of the following, the symbol shown at the right, as used in a systems flow chart, means

    A. document
    B. manual operation
    C. planning
    D. process

17. The mean age of a sample group drawn from population X is 37.5 years and the standard error of the mean is 5.9. There is a *99%* probability that the computed mean age of other samples drawn from population X would fall within the range of

    A. 31.6–43.4 B. 26.0–52.7
    C. 22.2–52.8 D. 20.0–55.0

18. After a budget has been developed, it serves to

    A. assist the accounting department in posting expenditures
    B. measure the effectiveness of department managers
    C. provide a yardstick against which actual costs are measured
    D. provide the operating department with total expenditures to date

19. In order to ensure that work measurement or time study results will be consistent from one study to another, and reflect a fair day's work, the performance of the clerks must be rated or levelled.
    Which of the following is LEAST likely to be included among the techniques for determining the performance level or for rating the study?

    A. Predetermined times B. Published rating tables
    C. Sampling studies   D. Training films

20. Of the following, the BEST practice to follow when training a new employee is to

    A. encourage him to feel free to ask questions at any time
    B. immediately demonstrate how fast his job can be done so he will know what is expected of him
    C. let him watch other employees for a week or two
    D. point out mistakes after completion so he will learn by experience

21. An IMPORTANT aspect to keep in mind during the decision-making process is that

    A. all possible alternatives for attaining goals should be sought out and considered
    B. considering various alternatives only leads to confusion
    C. once a decision has been made, it cannot be retracted
    D. there is only one correct method to reach any goal

22. Implementation of accountability REQUIRES

    A. a leader who will not hesitate to take punitive action
    B. an established system of communication from the bottom to the top
    C. explicit directives from leaders
    D. too much expense to justify it

23. Of the following, the MAJOR difference between systems and procedures analysis and work simplification is:

    A. The former complicates organizational routine and the latter simplifies it
    B. The former is objective and the latter is subjective
    C. The former generally utilizes expert advice and the latter is a *do-it-yourself* improvement by supervisors and workers
    D. There is no difference other than in name

24. Systems development is concerned with providing

    A. a specific set of work procedures
    B. an overall framework to describe general relationships
    C. definitions of particular organizational functions
    D. organizational symbolism

25. Organizational systems and procedures should be

    A. developed as problems arise as no design can anticipate adequately the requirements of an organization
    B. developed jointly by experts in systems and procedures and the people who are responsible for implementing them
    C. developed solely by experts in systems and procedures
    D. eliminated whenever possible to save unnecessary expense

26. The CHIEF danger of a decentralized control system is that

    A. excessive reports and communications will be generated
    B. problem areas may not be detected readily
    C. the expense will become prohibitive
    D. this will result in too many *chiefs*

27. Of the following, management guides and controls clerical work PRINCIPALLY through

    A. close supervision and constant checking of personnel
    B. spot checking of clerical procedures
    C. strong sanctions for clerical supervisors
    D. the use of printed forms

28. Which of the following is MOST important before conducting fact-finding interviews?

    A. Becoming acquainted with all personnel to be interviewed
    B. Explaining the techniques you plan to use
    C. Explaining to the operating officials the purpose and scope of the study
    D. Orientation of the physical layout

29. Of the following, the one that is NOT essential in carrying out a comprehensive work improvement program is

    A. standards of performance
    B. supervisory training
    C. work count/task list
    D. work distribution chart

30. Which of the following control techniques is MOST useful on large, complex systems projects?

    A. A general work plan   B. Gantt chart
    C. Monthly progress report   D. PERT chart

31. The action which is MOST effective in gaining acceptance of a study by the agency which is being studied is

    A. a directive from the agency head to install a study based on recommendations included in a report
    B. a lecture-type presentation following approval of the procedures
    C. a written procedure in narrative form covering the proposed system with visual presentations and discussions
    D. procedural charts showing the *before* situation, forms, steps, etc. to the employees affected

32. Which of the following is NOT an advantage in the use of oral instructions as compared with written instructions? Oral instruction(s)

    A. can easily be changed
    B. is superior in transmitting complex directives
    C. facilitate exchange of information between a superior and his subordinate
    D. with discussions make it easier to ascertain understanding

33. Which organization principle is MOST closely related to procedural analysis and improvement?

    A. Duplication, overlapping, and conflict should be eliminated.
    B. Managerial authority should be clearly defined.
    C. The objectives of the organization should be clearly defined.
    D. Top management should be freed of burdensome detail.

34. Which one of the following is the MAJOR objective of operational audits?

    A. Detecting fraud
    B. Determining organization problems
    C. Determining the number of personnel needed
    D. Recommending opportunities for improving operating and management practices

35. Of the following, the formalization of organization structure is BEST achieved by
    A. a narrative description of the plan of organization
    B. functional charts
    C. job descriptions together with organization charts
    D. multi-flow charts

36. Budget planning is MOST useful when it achieves
    A. cost control
    B. forecast of receipts
    C. performance review
    D. personnel reduction

37. The UNDERLYING principle of sound administration is to
    A. base administration on investigation of facts
    B. have plenty of resources available
    C. hire a strong administrator
    D. establish a broad policy

38. Although questionnaires are not the best survey tool the management analyst has to use, there are times when a good questionnaire can expedite the *fact-finding* phase of a management survey.
    Which of the following should be AVOIDED in the design and distribution of the questionnaire?
    A. Questions should be framed so that answers can be classified and tabulated for analysis.
    B. Those receiving the questionnaire must be knowledgeable enough to accurately provide the information desired.
    C. The questionnaire should enable the respondent to answer in a narrative manner.
    D. The questionnaire should require a minimum amount of writing.

39. Of the following, the formula which is used to calculate the arithmetic mean from data grouped in a frequency distribution is:
    M =

    A. $\dfrac{n}{\Sigma fx}$
    B. $N(\Sigma fx)$
    C. $\dfrac{\Sigma fx}{N}$
    D. $\dfrac{\Sigma x}{fN}$

40. Arranging large groups of numbers in frequency distributions
    A. gives a more composite picture of the total group than a random listing
    B. is misleading in most cases
    C. is unnecessary in most instances
    D. presents the data in a form whereby further manipulation of the group is eliminated

KEY (CORRECT ANSWERS)

1. B	11. A	21. A	31. C
2. C	12. A	22. B	32. B
3. D	13. C	23. C	33. A
4. A	14. C	24. B	34. D
5. C	15. D	25. B	35. C
6. C	16. B	26. B	36. A
7. A	17. C	27. D	37. A
8. B	18. C	28. C	38. C
9. A	19. C	29. B	39. C
10. A	20. A	30. D	40. A

EXAMINATION SECTION
TEST 1

DIRECTIONS: Each question or incomplete statement is followed by several suggested answers or completions. Select the one that BEST answers the question or completes the statement. *PRINT THE LETTER OF THE CORRECT ANSWER IN THE SPACE AT THE RIGHT.*

1. In performing a systems study, the analyst may find it necessary to prepare an accurate record of working statistics from departmental forms, questionnaires, and information gleaned in interviews.
   Which one of the following statements dealing with the statistical part of the study is the MOST valid?

    A. The emphasis of every survey is data collection.
    B. Data should not be represented in narrative form.
    C. The statistical report should include the titles of personnel required for each processing task.
    D. In gathering facts, the objective of a systems study should be the primary consideration

2. The most direct method of obtaining information about activities in the area under study is by observation. There are several general rules for an analyst that are essential for observing and being accepted as an observer.
   The one of the following statements relating to this aspect of an analyst's responsibility that is most valid in the initial phase is that the analyst should NOT

    A. limit himself to observing only; he may criticize operations and methods
    B. prepare himself for what he is about to observe
    C. obtain permission of the department's management to actually perform some of the clerical tasks himself
    D. offer views of impending charges regarding new staff requirements, equipment, or procedures

3. The active concern of the systems analyst is the study and documentation of what he observes as it exists. Before attempting the actual study and documentation, the analyst should comply with certain generally accepted procedures.
   Of the following, the step the analyst should *generally lake* FIRST is to

    A. define the problem and prepare a statement of objectives
    B. confer with the project director concerning persons to be interviewed
    C. accumulate data from all available sources within the area under study
    D. meet with operations managers to enlist their cooperation

4. During the course of any systems study, the analyst will have to gather some statistics if the operation model is to be realistic and meaningful.
   With respect to the statistical report part of the study, it is MOST valid to say that

A. it must follow a standard format since there should be no variation from one study to the next
B. the primary factor to be considered is the volume of work in the departmental unit at each stage of completion
C. only variations that occur during peak and slow periods should be recorded
D. unless deadlines in the departmental units studied by the analyst occur constantly, they should not be taken into account

5. In systems analysis, the interview is one of the analyst's major sources of information. In conducting an interview, he should strive for immediate rapport with the operations manager or department head with whom he deals.
With respect to his responsibility in this area, it is considered LEAST appropriate for the analyst to

   A. explain the full background of the study and the scope of the investigation
   B. emphasize the importance of achieving the stated objectives and review the plan of the project
   C. assume that the attitudes of the workers are less important than those of the executives
   D. request the manager's assistance in the form of questions, suggestions, and general cooperation

6. Large, complex endeavors often take a long time to implement. The following statements relate to long lead times imposed by large-scale endeavors.
Select the one usually considered to be LEAST valid.

   A. Where there are external sponsors who provide funds or political support, they should be provided with some demonstration of what is being accomplished.
   B. Long lead times simplify planning and diminish the threat of obsolescence by assuring that objectives will be updated by the time the project is nearing completion.
   C. During the period when no tangible results are forthcoming, techniques must be found to assess progress.
   D. Employees, particularly scientific personnel, should feel a sense of accomplishment or they may shy away from research which involves long-term commitments.

7. In traditional management theory, administrators are expected to collect and weigh facts and probabilities, make an optimal decision and see that it is carried out.
In the management of large-scale development projects, such a clear sequence of action is *generally* NOT possible because of

   A. their limited duration
   B. the static and fixed balance of power among interest groups
   C. continuous suppression of new facts
   D. constantly changing constraints and pressures

Questions 8-10.

DIRECTIONS: One of the most valuable parts of the systems package is the systems flowchart, a technique that aids understanding of the work flow. A flowchart should depict all the intricacies of the work flow from start to finish in order to give the onlooker a solid picture at a glance. The table below contains symbols used by the analyst in flowcharting. In answering Questions 8 through 10, refer to the following figures.

Figure I
Figure II 
Figure III
Figure IV 
Figure V
Figure VI 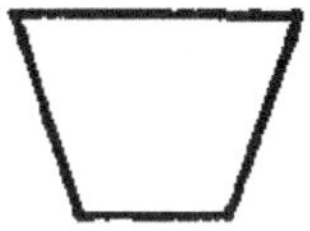
Figure VII
Figure VIII
Figure IX
Figure X
Figure XI
Figure XII
Figure XIII

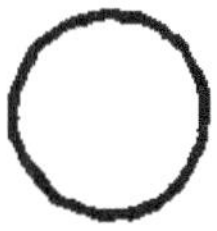

8. The symbol that is COMMONLY used to specify clerical procedures which are not essential to the main processing function and yet are part of the overall procedure is represented by Figure

   A. III　　　B. VI　　　C. XII　　　D. XIII

9. An analyst wishes to designate the following activities:
   File reports; Calculate average; Attach labels.
   The MOST APPROPRIATE symbol to use is represented by Figure

   A. V　　　B. VI　　　C. VII　　　D. II

10. A *Report, Journal,* or *Record* should be represented by Figure

    A. I　　　B. III　　　C. IX　　　D. XI

Question 11.

DIRECTIONS: The following figures are often used in program and systems flowcharting.

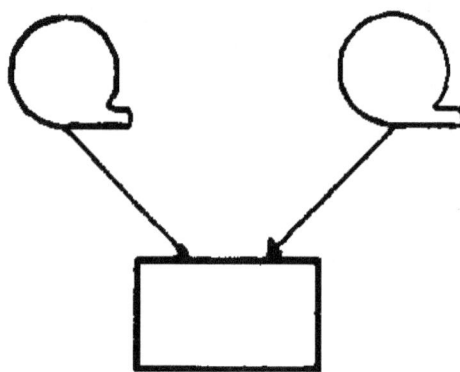

11. The above figures represent

    A. two storage discs incorporated in a processing function
    B. two report papers to be put in a cabinet in chronological order
    C. two transmittal tapes—both externally generated—routed to a vault
    D. an auxiliary operation involving two sequential decisions

12. When research and analysis of government programs, e.g., pest control, drug rehabilitation, etc., is sponsored and conducted within a government unit, the scope of the analysis should *generally* be _____ the scope of the authority of the manager to whom the analyst is responsible.

    A. less than
    B. less than or equal to
    C. greater than or equal to
    D. greater than

13. In recent years, there has been an increasing emphasis on outputs—the goods and services that a program produces. This emphasis on outputs imposes an information requirement. The one of the following which would MOST likely NOT be considered output information in a hospital or health care program is the

    A. number of patients cared for
    B. number of days patients were hospitalized
    C. budgeted monies for hospital beds
    D. quality of the service

14. Which one of the following statements pertaining to management information systems is generally considered to be LEAST valid?

    A. A management information system is a network of related subsystems developed according to an integrated scheme for evaluating the activities of an agency.
    B. A management information system specifies the content and format, the preparation and integration of information for all various functions within an agency that will best satisfy needs at various levels of management.
    C. To operate a successful management information system, an agency will require a complex electronic computer installation.
    D. The five elements which compose a management information system are: data input, files, data processing, procedures, and data output.

15. In the field of records management, electronic equipment is being used to handle office paperwork or data processing. With respect to such use, of the following, it is MOST valid to say that

    A. electronic equipment is not making great strides in the achievement of speed and economy in office paperwork
    B. electronic equipment accelerates the rate at which office paperwork is completed
    C. paperwork problems can be completely solved through mechanization
    D. introduction of electronic data processing equipment cuts down on the paper consumed in office processes

16. A reports control program evaluates the reporting requirements of top management so that reviews can be made of the existing reporting system to determine its adequacy. Of the following statements pertaining to reports control, which is the MOST likely to be characteristic of such a program?

    A. Only the exception will be reported
    B. Preparation of daily reports will be promoted
    C. Executives will not delegate responsibility for preparing reports
    D. Normal conditions are reported

17. Which of the following types of work measurement techniques requires the HIGHEST degree of training and skill of technicians and supervisors and is MOST likely to involve the HIGHEST original cost?

    A. Work sampling
    B. Predetermined time standards
    C. The time study (stopwatch timing)
    D. Employee reporting

18. Which of the following types of work measurement techniques *generally* requires the LEAST amount of time to measure and establish standards?

    A. Work sampling
    B. Predetermined time standards
    C. The time study (stopwatch timing)
    D. Employee reporting

19. Assume that you, as an analyst, have been assigned to formally organize small work groups within a city department to perform a special project. After studying the project, you find you must choose between two possible approaches—either task teams or highly functionalized groups.
    What would be one of the advantages of choosing the task-team approach over the highly functionalized organization?

    A. Detailed, centralized planning would be encouraged.
    B. Indifference to city goals and restrictions on output would be lessened.
    C. Work would be divided into very specialized areas.
    D. Superiors would be primarily concerned with seeing that subordinates do not deviate from the project.

20. In systems theory, there is a *what-if* method of treating uncertainty that explores the effect on the alternatives of environmental change. This method is generally referred to as _____ analysis.

   A. sensitivity
   B. contingency
   C. a fortiori
   D. systems

KEY (CORRECT ANSWERS)

1. D
2. D
3. A
4. B
5. C
6. B
7. D
8. D
9. A
10. B

11. A
12. B
13. C
14. C
15. B
16. A
17. B
18. A
19. B
20. B

TEST 2

DIRECTIONS: Each question or incomplete statement is followed by several suggested answers or completions. Select the one that BEST answers the question or completes the statement. *PRINT THE LETTER OF THE CORRECT ANSWER IN THE SPACE AT THE RIGHT.*

1. Which of the following systems exists at the strategic level of an organization?

    A. Decision support system (DSS)
    B. Executive support system (ESS)
    C. Knowledge work system (KWS)
    D. Management information system (MIS)

2. The functions of knowledge workers in an organization generally include each of the following EXCEPT

    A. updating knowledge
    B. managing documentation of knowledge
    C. serving as internal consultants
    D. acting as change agents

3. Which of the following is not a management benefit associated with end-user development of information systems?

    A. Reduced application backlog
    B. Increased user satisfaction
    C. Simplified testing and documentation procedures
    D. Improved requirements determination

4. Assume that an analyst is preparing an analysis of a departmental program. His investigation leads him to a potential problem relating to the program. The analyst thinks the potential problem is so serious that he cannot rely on preventive actions to remove the cause or significantly reduce the probability of its occurrence.
    Of the following, the MOST appropriate way for the analyst to promptly handle this serious matter described above would be to

    A. apply systematic afterthought to the achievement of objectives by analysis of the problem
    B. compare actual performance with the expected standard of performance
    C. prepare contingency actions to be adopted immediately if the problem does occur
    D. identify, locate, and describe the deviation from the standard

5. Assume that an analyst is directed to investigate a problem relating to organizational behavior in his agency and to prepare a report thereon. After reviewing the preliminary draft, his superior cautions him to overcome his tendency to misuse and overgeneralize his interpretation of existing knowledge.
    Which one of the following statements appearing in the draft is MOST *usually* considered to be a common distortion of behavioral science knowledge?

    A. Pay—even incentive pay—isn't very important anymore.
    B. There are nonrational aspects to people's behavior.
    C. The informal system exerts much control over organizational participants.
    D. Employees have many motives.

Questions 6-10.

DIRECTIONS: Each of Questions 6 through 10 consists of a statement which contains one word that is incorrectly used because it is not in keeping with the meaning that the quotation is evidently intended to convey. Determine which word is incorrectly used. Then select from the words lettered A, B, C, or D the word which, when substituted for the incorrectly used word, would BEST help to convey the meaning of the statement.

6. While the utilization of cost-benefit analysis in decision-making processes should be encouraged, it must be well understood that there are many limitations on the constraints of the analysis. One must be cautioned against using cost-benefit procedures automatically and blindly. Still, society will almost certainly be better off with the application of cost-benefit methods than it would be without them. As some authorities aptly point out, an important advantage of a cost-benefit study is that it forces those responsible to quantify costs and benefits as far as possible rather than rest content with vague qualitative judgments or personal hunches. Also, such an analysis has the very valuable byproduct of causing questions to be asked which would otherwise not have been raised. Finally, even if cost-benefit analysis cannot give the right answer, it can sometimes play the purely negative role of screening projects and rejecting those answers which are obviously less promising.

    A. precise
    B. externally
    C. applicability
    D. unresponsiveness

7. The programming method used by the government should attempt to assess the costs and benefits of individual projects, in comparison with private and other public alternatives. The program, then, consists of the most meritorious projects that the budget will design. Meritorious projects excluded from the budget provide arguments for increasing its size. There are difficulties inherent in the specific project approach. The attempt is to apply profit criteria in public projects analogous to those used in evaluating private projects. This involves comparison of monetary values of present and future costs and benefits. But, in many important cases, such as highways, parkways, and bridges, the product of the government's investment does not directly enter the market economy. Consequently, evaluation requires imputation of market values. For example, the returns on a bridge have been estimated by attempting to value the time saved by users. Such measurements necessarily contain a strong, element of artificiality.

    A. annulled   B. expedient   C. accommodate   D. marginally

8. Consider the problem of budgeting for activities designed to alleviate poverty and rooted unemployment. Are skill retraining efforts better or worse investments than public works? Are they better or worse than subsidies or other special incentives to attract new industry? Or, at an even more fundamental level, is a dollar invested in an attempt to rehabilitate a mature, technologically displaced, educationally handicapped, unemployed man a better commitment than a comparable dollar invested in supporting the educational and technical preparation of his son for employment in a different line of work? The questions may look unreasonable, even unanswerable. But the fact is that they are implicitly answered in any budget decision in the defined problem area. The only subordinate issue is whether the answer rests on intuition and guess, or on a budget system that presents relevant information so organized as to contribute to rational analysis, planning, and decision-making.

    A. incomplete
    B. relevant
    C. significant
    D. speculate

9. Choices among health programs, on the basis of cost-benefit analysis, raise another set of ethical problems. Measuring discounted lifetime earnings does not reveal the value of alleviating pain and suffering; some diseases have a high death rate, others are debilitating, others are merely uncomfortable. In general, choices among health and education programs that are predicated on discounted lifetime earnings will structure the choice against those who have low earnings, those whose earnings will materialize only at some future point in time, or those whose participation in the labor force is limited. It may be an appropriate economic policy to reduce expenditures in areas that maximize the future level of national income. But the maximization of social welfare may dictate attention to considerations, such as equality of opportunity, that transcend the limitations of values defined in such narrow terms.

    A. concentrate   B. divergent   C. enforcing   D. favorably

10. Without defined and time-phased objectives, it is difficult to be critical of administrative performance. To level a charge of waste or malperformance at the managers of a public program is, of course, one of the more popular pastimes of any administration's loyal opposition. But it is a rare experience to find such a charge documented by the kind of precise cost-effectiveness measures that are the common test of the quality of management performance in a well-run organization. Those who take a professional view of management responsibility are even more concerned about the acceptance of the kind of information that would enable a manager to assess the progress and quality of his own performance and, as appropriate, to initiate corrective action before outside criticism can even start.

    A. absence   B. rebut   C. withdraw   D. impeded

11. What is the relationship between the cost of inputs and the value of outputs when the results obtained from a program can be measured in money? _____ ratio.

    A. Value administrative-cost   B. Break-even point
    C. Variable-direct   D. Cost-benefit

12. Some writers in the field of public expenditure have noted a disturbing tendency inherent in cost-benefit analysis. Which one of the following statements MOST accurately expresses their concern over the use of cost-benefit analysis? It

    A. encourages the attachment of monetary values to intangibles
    B. has a built-in neglect of measurable outcomes while emphasizing the nonmeasurable
    C. consciously exaggerates social values and overstates political values
    D. encourages emphasis of those costs and benefits that cannot be measured rather than those that can

13. In private industry, budgetary control begins logically with an estimate of sales and the income therefrom.
    Of the following, the term used in government which is MOST analogous to that of sales in private industry is

    A. borrowed funds   B. the amount appropriated
    C. general overhead   D. surplus funds

14. When constructing graphs of causally related variables, how should the variables be placed to conform to conventional use?

    A. The independent variable should be placed on the vertical axis and the dependent variable on the horizontal axis.
    B. The dependent variable should be placed on the vertical axis and the independent variable on the horizontal axis.
    C. Independent variables should be placed on both axes.
    D. Dependent variables should be placed on both axes.

Questions 15-18.

DIRECTIONS: Answer Questions 15 through 18 on the basis of the following graph describing the output of computer operators.

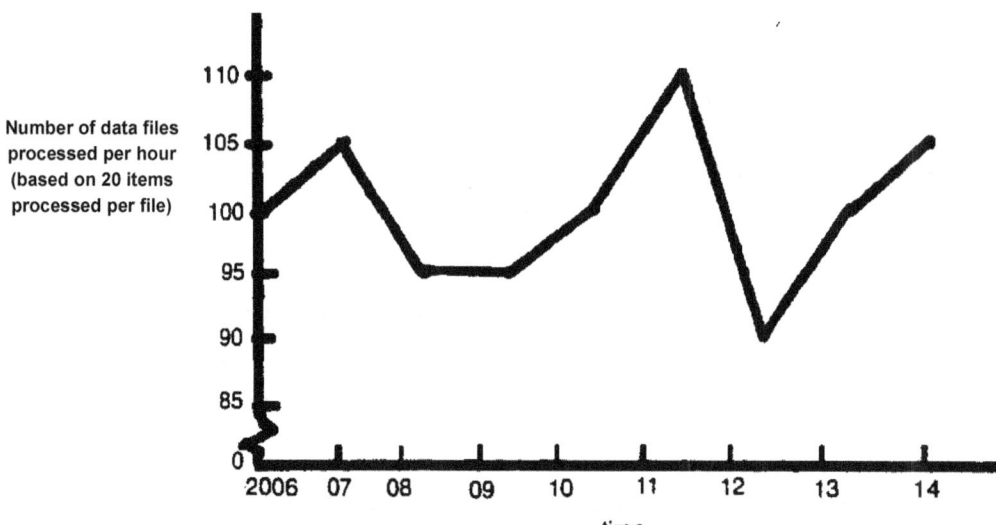

15. Of the following, during what four-year period did the AVERAGE OUTPUT of computer operators *fall below* 100 data files per hour?

    A. 2007-10   B. 2008-11   C. 2010-13   D. 2011-14

16. The AVERAGE PERCENTAGE CHANGE in output over the previous year's output for the years 2009 to 2012 is MOST NEARLY

    A. 2   B. 0   C. -5   D. -7

17. The DIFFERENCE between the actual output for 2012 and the projected figure based upon the average increase from 2006 to 2011 is MOST NEARLY

    A. 18   B. 20   C. 22   D. 24

18. Assume that after constructing the above graph, you, an analyst, discovered that the average number of items processed per file in 2012 was 25 (instead of 20) because of the complex nature of the work performed during that period.
    The AVERAGE OUTPUT in files per hour for the period 2010 to 2013, expressed in terms of 20 items per file, would then be APPROXIMATELY

    A. 95 B. 100 C. 105 D. 110

19. Assume that Unit S's production fluctuated substantially from one year to another. In 2009, Unit S's production was 100% greater than in 2008; in 2010, it was 25% less than in 2009; and in 2011, it was 10% greater than in 2010. On the basis of this information, it is CORRECT to conclude that Unit S's production in 2011 exceeded its production in 2008 by

    A. 50% B. 65% C. 75% D. 90%

20. Statistical sampling is often used in administrative operations primarily because it enables

    A. administrators to make staff selections
    B. decisions to be made based on mathematical and scientific fact
    C. courses of action to be determined by electronic data processing or computer programs
    D. useful predictions to be made from relatively small samples

KEY (CORRECT ANSWERS)

1. B
2. B
3. C
4. C
5. A

6. C
7. C
8. C
9. A
10. A

11. D
12. A
13. B
14. B
15. A

16. B
17. C
18. C
19. B
20. D

EXAMINATION SECTION
TEST 1

DIRECTIONS: Each question or incomplete statement is followed by several suggested answers or completions. Select the one that BEST answers the question or completes the statement. *PRINT THE LETTER OF THE CORRECT ANSWER IN THE SPACE AT THE RIGHT*

1. Of the following, the BEST statement concerning the placement of *Conclusions and Recommendations* in a management report is:

    A. Recommendations should always be included in a report unless the report presents the results of an investigation
    B. If a report presents conclusions, it must present recommendations
    C. Every statement that is a conclusion should grow out of facts given elsewhere in the report
    D. Conclusions and recommendations should always conclude the report because they depend on its contents

2. Assume you are preparing a systematic analysis of your agency's pest control program and its effect on eliminating rodent infestation of premises in a specific region.
   To omit from your report important facts which you originally received from the person to whom you are reporting is GENERALLY considered to be

    A. *desirable;* anyone who is likely to read the report can consult his files for extra information
    B. *undesirable;* the report should include major facts that are obtained as a result of your efforts
    C. *desirable;* the person you are reporting to does not
    D. pass the report on to others who lack his own familiarity with the subject
    E. *undesirable;* the report should include all of the facts that are obtained as a result of your efforts

3. Of all the nonverbal devices used in report writing, tables are used most frequently to enable a reader to compare statistical information more easily. Hence, it is important that an analyst know when to use tables.
   Which one of the following statements that relate to tables is generally considered to be LEAST valid?

    A. A table from an outside source must be acknowledged by the report writer.
    B. A table should be placed far in advance of the point where it is referred to or discussed in the report.
    C. The notes applying to a table are placed at the bottom of the table, rather than at the bottom of the page on which the table is found.
    D. A table should indicate the major factors that effect the data it contains.

4. Assume that an analyst writes reports which contain more detail than might be needed to serve their purpose.
   Such a practice is GENERALLY considered to be

A. *desirable;* this additional detail permits maximized machine utilization
B. *undesirable;* if specifications of reports are defined when they are first set up, loss of flexibility will follow
C. *desirable;* everything ought to be recorded so it will be there if it is ever needed
D. *undesirable;* recipients of these reports are likely to discredit them entirely

5. Assume that an analyst is gathering certain types of information which can be obtained only through interrogation of the clientele by means of a questionnaire.
Which one of the following statements that relate to construction of the questionnaire is the MOST valid?

   A. Stress, whenever possible, the use of leading questions.
   B. Avoid questions which touch on personal prejudice or pride.
   C. Opinions, as much as facts, should be sought.
   D. There is no psychological advantage for starting with a question of high interest value.

Questions 6-10.

DIRECTIONS: Questions 6 through 10 consist of sentences lettered A, B, C, and D. For each question, choose the sentence which is stylistically and grammatically MOST appropriate for a management report.

6. A. For too long, the citizen has been forced to rely for his productivity information on the whims, impressions and uninformed opinion of public spokesmen.
   B. For too long, the citizen has been forced to base his information about productivity on the whims, impressions and uninformed opinion of public spokesmen.
   C. The citizen has been forced to base his information about productivity on the whims, impressions and uninformed opinion of public spokesmen for too long.
   D. The citizen has been forced for too long to rely for his productivity information on the whims, impressions and uninformed opinion of public spokesmen.

7. A. More competition means lower costs to the city, thereby helping to compensate for inflation.
   B. More competition, helping to compensate for inflation, means lower costs to the city.
   C. Inflation may be compensated for by more competition, which will reduce the city's costs.
   D. The costs to the city will be lessened by more competition, helping to compensate for inflation.

8. A. Some objectives depend on equal efforts from others, particularly private interests and the federal government; for example, technical advancement.
   B. Some objectives, such as technical advancement, depend on equal efforts from others, particularly private interests and the federal government.
   C. Some objectives depend on equal efforts from others, particularly private interests and the federal government, such as technical advancement.
   D. Some objectives depend on equal efforts from others (technical advancement, for example); particularly private interests and the federal government.

9. A. It has always been the practice of this office to effectuate recruitment of prospective employees from other departments.
    B. This office has always made a practice of recruiting prospective employees from other departments.
    C. Recruitment of prospective employees from other departments has always been a practice which has been implemented by this office.
    D. Implementation of the policy of recruitment of prospective employees from other departments has always been a practice of this office.

10. A. These employees are assigned to the level of work evidenced by their efforts and skills during the training period.
    B. The level of work to which these employees is assigned is decided upon on the basis of the efforts and skills evidenced by them during the period in which they were trained.
    C. Assignment of these employees is made on the basis of the level of work their efforts and skills during the training period has evidenced.
    D. These employees are assigned to a level of work their efforts and skills during the training period have evidenced.

11. To overcome the manual collation problem, forms are frequently padded. Of the following statements which relate to this type of packaging, select the one that is MOST accurate.

    A. Typewritten forms which are prepared as padded forms are more efficient than all other packaging.
    B. Padded forms are best suited for handwritten forms.
    C. It is difficult for a printer to pad form copies of different colors.
    D. Registration problems increase when cut-sheet forms are padded.

12. Most forms are cut from a standard mill sheet of paper.
    This is the size on which forms dealers base their prices. Since an agency is paying for a full-size sheet of paper, it is the responsibility of the analyst to design forms so that as many as possible may be cut from the sheet without waste.
    Of the following sizes, select the one that will cut from a standard mill sheet with the GREATEST waste and should, therefore, be avoided if possible.

    A. 4" x 6"   B. 5" x 8"   C. 9" x 12"   D. 8 1/2" x 14"

13. Assume that you are assigned the task of reducing the time and costs involved in completing a form that is frequently used in your agency. After analyzing the matter, you decide to reduce the writing requirements of the form through the use of ballot boxes and preprinted data.
    If exact copy-to-copy registration of this form is necessary, it is MOST advisable to

    A. vary the sizes of the ballot boxes
    B. stagger the ballot boxes
    C. place the ballot boxes as close together as possible
    D. have the ballot boxes follow the captions

14. To overcome problems that are involved in the use of cut-sheet and padded forms, specialty forms have been developed. Normally, these forms are commercially manufactured rather than produced in-plant. Before designing a form as a specialty form, however, you should be assured that certain factors are present.
Which one of the following factors deserves LEAST consideration?

    A. The form is to be used in quantities of 5,000 or more annually.
    B. The forms will be prepared on equipment using either a pinfeed device or pressure rollers for continuous feed-through.
    C. Two or more copies of the form set must be held together for further processing subsequent to the initial distribution of the form set.
    D. Copies of the form will be identical and no items of data will be selectively eliminated from one or more copies of the form.

15. Although a well-planned form should require little explanation as to its completion, there are many occasions when the analyst will find it necessary to include instructions on the form to assure that the person completing it does so correctly.
With respect to such instructions, it is usually considered to be LEAST appropriate to place them

    A. in footnotes at the bottom of the form
    B. following the spaces to be completed
    C. directly under the form's title
    D. on the front of the form

16. One of the basic data-arrangement methods used in forms design is the *on-line* method. When this method is used, captions appear on the same line as the space provided for entry of the variable data.
This arrangement is NOT recommended because it

    A. forces the typist to make use of document tabs, thus increasing processing time
    B. wastes horizontal space since the caption appears on the writing line
    C. tends to make the variable data become more dominant than the captions
    D. increases the form's processing time by requiring the typist to continually alter margins and indents

17. Before designing a form for his agency, the analyst should be aware of certain basic design standards.
Which one of the following statements relating to horizontal and vertical spacing requirements is *generally* considered to be the MOST acceptable in forms design?

    A. If the form will be completed by computer, no more than four writing lines to the vertical inch should be allowed.
    B. If the form will be completed by hand, allowance should not be made for the different sizes of individual handwriting.
    C. If the form will be completed partly by hand and partly by computer, the analyst should provide the same vertical spacing as for typewriter completion
    D. The form should be designed with proportional spacing for pica and elite type.

18. As an analyst, you may be required to conduct a functional analysis of your agency's forms.
    Which one of the following statements pertaining to this type of analysis is *generally* considered to be MOST valid?

    A. Except for extremely low-volume forms, all forms should be functionally analyzed.
    B. To obtain maximum benefit from the analysis, functional re-analyses of all forms should be undertaken at least once every three to six months.
    C. All existing forms should be functionally analyzed before reorder.
    D. Only new forms should be functionally analyzed prior to being authorized for adoption.

19. The analyst must assure the users of a form that its construction provides for the most efficient method in terms of how data will be entered and processed subsequent to their initial entry.
    While the simplest construction is the cut sheet, the GREATEST disadvantage of this type of construction is

    A. the non-productive *makeready time* required if multiple copies of a form must be simultaneously prepared
    B. the difficulty experienced by users in filling in the forms solely by mechanical means
    C. its uneconomical cost of production
    D. the restrictions of limitations placed on the utilization of a variety of substances which may be used in form composition

20. Assume you have designed a form which requires data to be entered on multiple copies simultaneously. A determination has not yet been made whether to order the form as interleaved-carbon form sets or as carbonless forms.
    The advantage of using carbonless forms is that they

    A. permit more readable copies to be made at a single writing
    B. average about 30 percent lower in price than conventional interleaved-carbon form sets
    C. provide greater security if the information entered on the form is classified
    D. are not subject to accidental imaging

KEY (CORRECT ANSWERS)

1.	C	11.	B
2.	B	12.	C
3.	B	13.	B
4.	D	14.	D
5.	B	15.	A
6.	B	16.	B
7.	A	17.	C
8.	B	18.	C
9.	B	19.	A
10.	A	20.	C

TEST 2

DIRECTIONS: Each question or incomplete statement is followed by several suggested answers or completions. Select the one that BEST answers the question or completes the statement. *PRINT THE LETTER OF THE CORRECT ANSWER IN THE SPACE AT THE RIGHT.*

1. Many analysts lean toward the use of varying colors of paper in a multiple-part form set to indicate distribution. This usage is GENERALLY considered to be

    A. *desirable;* it is more effective than using white paper for all copies and imprinting the distribution in the margin of the copy
    B. *undesirable;* colored inks should be used instead to indicate distribution in a multipart form set
    C. *desirable;* it will lead to lower costs of form production
    D. *undesirable;* it causes operational difficulties if the form is to be microfilmed or optically scanned

2. After a form has been reviewed and approved by the analyst, it should be given an identifying number. The following items pertain to the form number.
Which item is MOST appropriately included as a portion of the form number?

    A. Revision date
    B. Order quantity
    C. Retention period
    D. Organization unit responsible for the form

Questions 3-8.

DIRECTIONS: Questions 3 through 8 should be answered on the basis of the following information.

Assume that the figure at the top of the next page is a systems flowchart specifically prepared for the purchasing department of a large municipal agency. Some of the symbols in the flowchart are incorrectly used. The symbols are numbered.

33

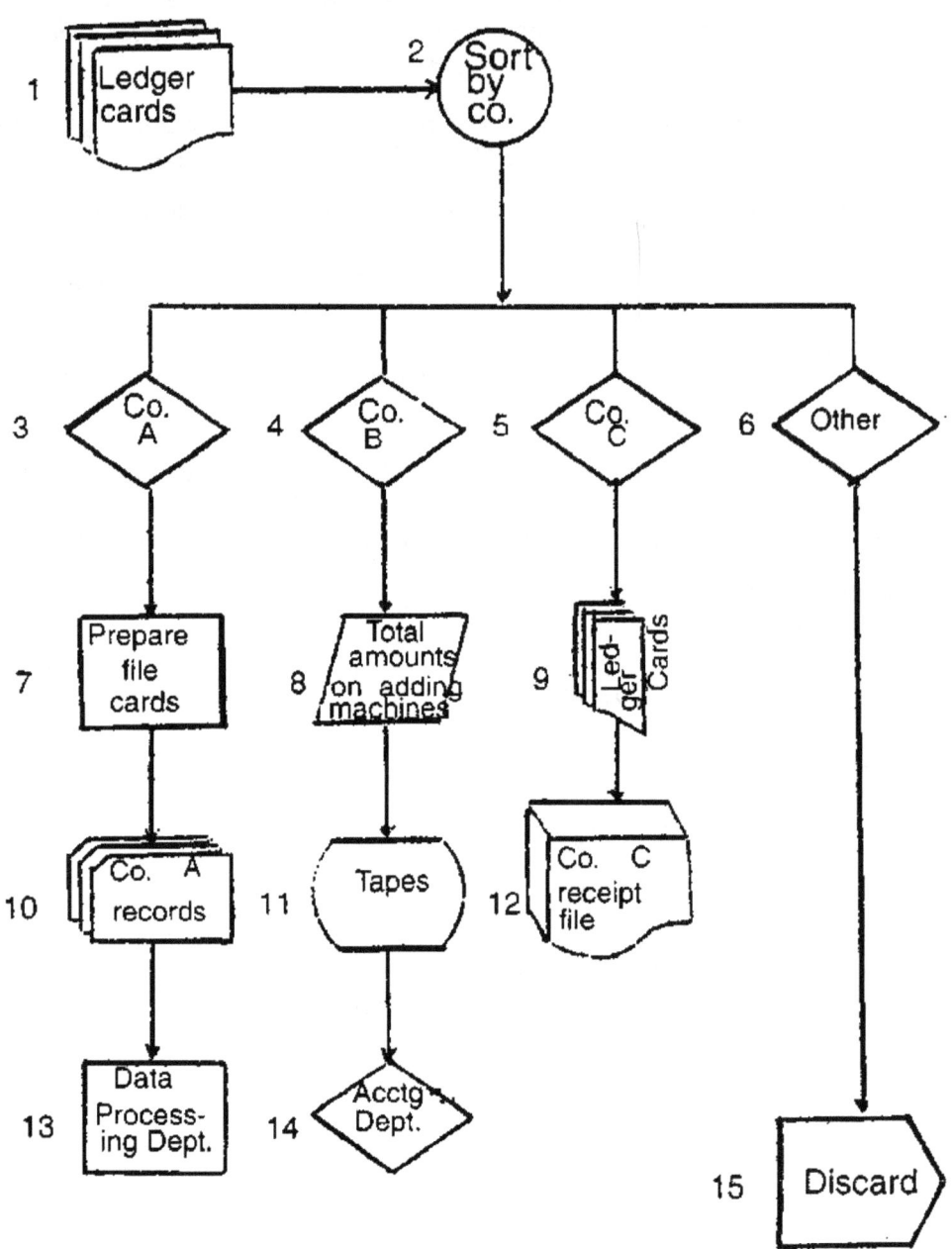

3. According to the flowchart, Number 2 is

   A. *correct*
   B. *incorrect;* the symbol should have six sides
   C. *incorrect;* the symbol should be the same as Number 7
   D. *incorrect;* the symbol should be the same as Number 8

4. According to the flowchart, Number 9 is

   A. *correct*
   B. *incorrect;* the symbol should be the same as Number 1

C. *incorrect;* the symbol should be the same as Number 7
D. *incorrect;* the symbol should be the same as Number 10

5. According to the flowchart, Number 11 is

   A. *Correct*
   B. *incorrect;* the symbol should be the same as Number 13
   C. *incorrect;* the symbol should be the same as Number 10
   D. *incorrect;* the symbol should be the same as Number 9

6. According to the flowchart, Number 14 is

   A. *correct*
   B. *incorrect;* the symbol should have three sides
   C. *incorrect;* the symbol should have six sides
   D. *incorrect;* the symbol should have eight sides

7. According to the flowchart, Number 12 is

   A. *Correct*
   B. *incorrect;* a *file* should be represented in the same form as the symbol which immediately precedes it
   C. *incorrect;* the symbol should be the same as Number 13
   D. *incorrect;* the symbol should be the same as Number 14

8. According to the flowchart, Number 15 is
   A. *correct*

   B. *incorrect;* the symbol should be

   C. *incorrect;* the symbol should be

   D. *incorrect;* the symbol should be

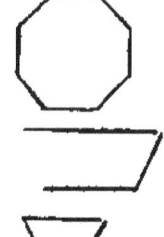

9. An agency expects to increase its services, the workload of the office will increase, and additional equipment and personnel will probably be required. Although there is no set formula for determining how much space will be required in an agency in a specific number of years from now, certain guidelines have been developed to assist the analyst in dealing with the problem of providing expansion space.
   Which of the following statements pertaining to this aspect of space utilization is *generally* considered to be the LEAST desirable practice?

   A. Spread the departments to fit into space that is temporarily surplus and awaiting the day when it is needed
   B. Place major departments where they can expand into the area of minor departments
   C. Visualize the direction in which the expansion will go and avoid placing the relatively fixed installations in the way
   D. Lay out the departments economically and screen off the surplus areas, using them for storage or other temporary usage

Questions 10-11.

DIRECTIONS: Questions 10 and 11 are based on the following layout.

Layout of Conference Room
BUREAU OF RODENT CONTROL

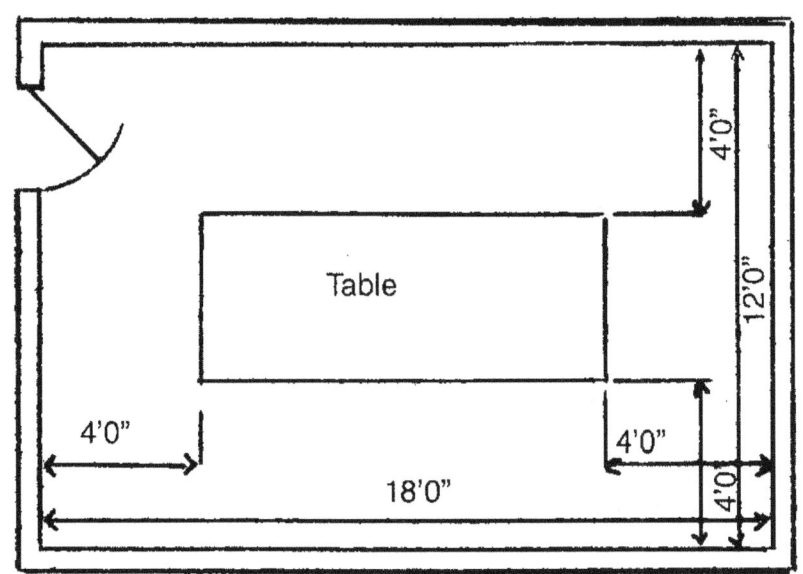

10. The LARGEST number of persons that can be accommodated in the area shown in the layout is
    A. 16   B. 10   C. 8   D. 6

11. Assume that the Bureau's programs undergo expansion and the Director indicates that the feasibility of increasing the size of the conference room should be explored.
    For every two additional persons that are to be accommodated, the analyst should recommend that _____ be added to table length and _____ be added to room length.

    A. 2'-6"; 2'-6"   B. 5'-0"; 5'-0"
    C. 2'-6"; 5'-0"   D. 5'-0"; 2'-6"

Questions 12-14.

DIRECTIONS: Questions 12 through 14 are based on the following information.

SYMBOLS USED IN LAYOUT WORK

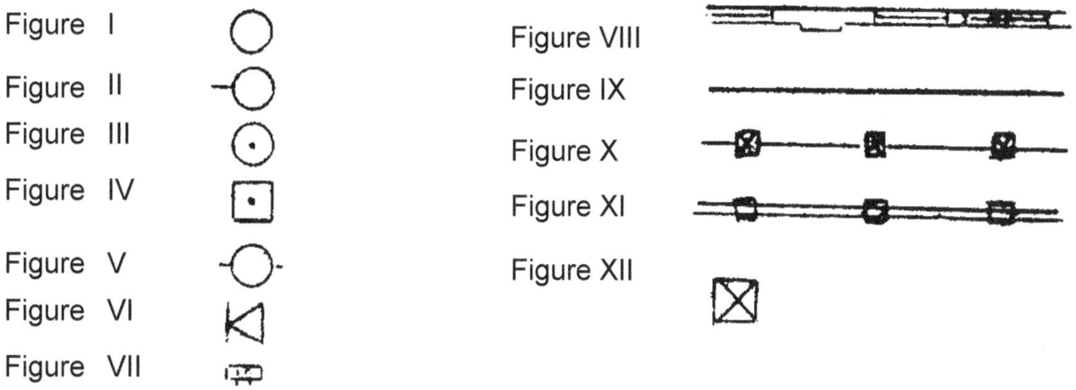

Figure I
Figure II
Figure III
Figure IV
Figure V
Figure VI
Figure VII
Figure VIII
Figure IX
Figure X
Figure XI
Figure XII

12. Figure XI is the symbol for

    A. a temporary partition
    B. floor outlets
    C. ceiling outlets
    D. a switch

13. A *solid post* is represented by Figure

    A. II   B. V   C. VIII   D. XII

14. Figure VI is the symbol for a(n)

    A. switch
    B. intercom
    C. telephone outlet
    D. railing

15. While there is no one office layout that will fit all organizations, there are some reasonably good principles of office layout by function that could be applied to any office situation. Which one of the following statements relating to functions and locations is MOST characteristic of a good layout?
    The

    A. personnel department is usually close to the reception area
    B. purchasing department should be far from the entrance
    C. data processing activity and duplicating services are normally placed together
    D. top management group is usually dispersed throughout the general office group

16. Records are valuable to an organization because recorded information is more accurate and enduring than oral information.
    Of the following, the MOST important stage in records management is at the

    A. storage stage
    B. time when quality control principles are applied
    C. point of distribution
    D. source when records are created

17. The rough layout of an office can be made by sketching the office floor plan from actual measurements, or it can be copied from blueprints furnished by the building management. As an analyst assigned to improve an office layout, you should be aware that the experienced layout man prefers to make his sketch from

    A. a blueprint because it eliminates the extra work in checking a sketch made from it
    B. actual measurements because a blueprint is in a scale of 1/4 or 1/2 inch to a foot instead of the preferred 1/8-inch scale
    C. a blueprint because he can always trust the blueprint
    D. actual measurements because he has to sketch in the desks and other equipment

18. Planning the traffic flow and appropriate aisle space in an office are factors an analyst must consider in any desk arrangement.
    Of the following, it is *generally the* MOST desirable practice to

    A. deny requests to rearrange desks to give employees more working space if the space left for the aisle is more than needed for the traffic
    B. figure operating space and the open file drawer separately from the allowance for the aisle if files must open into the aisle
    C. conserve space by making the main aisle in an office no wider than 36 inches
    D. disregard the length of feeders to an aisle in determining the width of the aisle

19. Code systems which are used to mark records for long- or short-term retention are easy to devise and use.
    Accordingly, of the following situations, it would be MOST appropriate to use the *destroy code* for

    A. information that calls for action within 90 days and for which no record is necessary thereafter
    B. information that may be needed for evaluation of past agency activities
    C. records which contain information that is readily available elsewhere
    D. records that contain information necessary for audit requirements

20. Assume your agency is moving into new quarters and you will assist your superior in assigning space to the various offices. The offices will be air-conditioned. The interior of the space to be assigned is located away from windows.
    Of the following, it is MOST appropriate for you to recommend that the interior of the space be set aside for

    A. legal offices and confidential investigation sections
    B. visitors to the agency
    C. conference and training rooms
    D. typing and stenographic pools

KEY (CORRECT ANSWERS)

1. D
2. A
3. A
4. B
5. D

6. C
7. A
8. C
9. A
10. B

11. A
12. A
13. D
14. C
15. A

16. D
17. D
18. B
19. C
20. C

EXAMINATION SECTION
TEST 1

DIRECTIONS: Each question or incomplete statement is followed by several suggested answers or completions. Select the one that BEST answers the question or completes the statement. *PRINT THE LETTER OF THE CORRECT ANSWER IN THE SPACE AT THE RIGHT.*

1. In organizational theory, the optimum span of control, that is, the number of subordinates who can be effectively supervised by one man above the level of the first line supervisor is GENERALLY set at between
    A. 3 and 6   B. 6 and 12   C. 12 and 18   D. 18 and 24

    1.____

2. Which of the following is LEAST desirable as a basic guide to normal conventional office layout?
    A. Arrange desks so that work flows in a normal fashion
    B. Place files nearest to the persons who will use them
    C. Utilize a number of small areas to provide privacy
    D. Utilize one single large area

    2.____

3. *A set of objects together with relationships between the objects and between their attributes* is the definition of
    A. a perceptual whole and its subcomponents
    B. a system in the terms of specific systems theory
    C. an organism
    D. forms control

    3.____

4. A technique of time study in which each employee maintains a record of his own time is GENERALLY known as _____ study.
    A. estimated time   B. observed time
    C. time log   D. wristwatch

    4.____

5. An employee has approached a supervisor with a request for a change involving his personal status or with a suggestion for making an improvement in the work The supervisor knows that the suggestion cannot be granted.
    Of the following, the BEST procedure would be for the supervisor to
    A. refer the matter to the personnel department
    B. refer the matter to his superior for action
    C. reject the proposal, explaining the defects or objections which cannot be overcome
    D. shelve the idea so that the employee will realize it cannot be acted upon

    5.____

6. There are, in general, a number of common methods of drawing samples for statistical work.
    The method in which a regularly ordered interval is maintained between the items chosen is BEST termed _____ sampling.
    A. random   B. stratified or selective
    C. systematic   D. work

    6.____

7. The multi-column process chart can be put to all of the following general uses EXCEPT to
   A. improve office layout
   B. improve procedures
   C. standardize procedures
   D. train personnel

8. If one wished to show the percentage of change over a period of time, the MOST appropriate type of graph or chart GENERALLY would be the _____ chart.
   A. bar
   B. line or curve
   C. logarithmic or semilogarithmic
   D. pie

9. A chart designed for the explicit purpose of portraying graphically information relating to the degree of responsibility of key individuals for the performance of various functions is BEST described as a(n) _____ chart.
   A. linear responsibility
   B. work distribution
   C. work process
   D. staff

10. The technique of work measurement LEAST useful for setting up a program of office incentive pay GENERALLY would be
    A. log sheets
    B. stopwatch time study
    C. wristwatch time study
    D. work sampling

11. There are a number of steps to be taken in making a work sampling study in order to set production standards. Three of the steps listed below are peculiar only to work sampling, in contrast with other work measurement techniques.
    The one EXCEPTION is:
    A. Define the breakdown of work into the proper elements of work and no-work or delay to be observed
    B. Determine the required number of observations needed for the specified degree of reliability
    C. Establish the observation intervals
    D. Make a preliminary estimate of work and no-work or delay element percentages for step A

12. A number of standardized flow process chart symbols have been generally accepted.
    The symbol $\bar{v}$ GENERALLY indicates a(n)
    A. delay
    B. storage or file
    C. inspection
    D. operation

13. The number of standardized flow process chart symbols have been generally accepted.
    The symbol ⊏⊐ GENERALLY indicates a(n)
    A. delay
    B. storage or file
    C. inspection
    D. operation

14. The type of work for which short interval scheduling generally would be LEAST applicable would be the work of a group of
    A. calculating clerks
    B. order clerks
    C. technically-oriented clerks
    D. typists

15. In writing a business report, the BEST expression to use, in general, of those listed below would NORMALLY be:
    A. Because
    B. Inasmuch as
    C. In view of the fact that
    D. With reference to

16. Of the following, the MAJOR advantage of a random access data processing system, as compared with a sequential-type system, is its
    A. ability to use more than one input system
    B. demand for more sophisticated systems and programming
    C. greater storage capacity and access speed
    D. potential for processing data on a *first come, first-served* basis

17. A good rule to remember with regard to decision making is that decisions should be made
    A. at the highest level competent to make such a decision
    B. at the lowest level competent to make such a decision
    C. by the person responsible for carrying out the decision
    D. by the person responsible for the work of the unit

18. Which of the following potential systems would LEAST likely be improved by being online? A(n) _____ system.
    A. budgeting control
    B. welfare eligibility
    C. employee payroll
    D. inventory control

19. A management information and control system essentially should be designed to provide management personnel with up-to-date information which will enable them to improve control over their operations.
    In designing such a system, the FIRST step to determine is:
    A. What information is needed to effectively control operations?
    B. What information is presently available?
    C. What organization changes are necessary to implement the system?
    D. Who is presently processing the information that might be used?

20. In designing control reports, which of the following guidelines is of MOST importance?
    A. Financial information should always be carried to the nearest penny.
    B. The report should be a simple and concise statement of only the pertinent facts.
    C. The report should indicate the source of original data and how the computations were made.
    D. The report should have the broadest possible distribution at all levels of management.

21. A situation which enables a number of users at offsite locations to have access to an office computer network is called
    A. multiprocessing
    B. multiprogramming
    C. cloud connectivity
    D. remote access

    21._____

22. Computer software that would typically be used for widespread dissemination of a business report is
    A. Microsoft Word
    B. Microsoft PowerPoint
    C. Adobe Elements
    D. Google Sheets

    22._____

23. Which of the following steps is LEAST desirable in designing an electronic data processing system?
    A. Design the EDP system first, then relate it to current operations
    B. Develop a corollary chart for the corresponding flow of information
    C. Develop a flow chart for the functions affected by the system
    D. Obtain from available EDP equipment that which best fits current operations

    23._____

24. Electronic data processing equipment can produce more information faster than can be generated by any other means. Because this is true, one wonders whether our ability to generate information has not far outstripped our ability to assimilate it.
    In view of this, a PERSISTENT danger management faces is in
    A. determining the budget for management information systems
    B. determining what information is of real worth
    C. finding enough computer personnel
    D. keeping their computers fully occupied

    24._____

25. The one of the following that is an ADVANTAGE of a hybrid local/remote network setup over fully local access is
    A. the ability to access a network outside normal circumstances
    B. closer oversight of personnel
    C. more efficient workflow
    D. reduced costs for software and production equipment

    25._____

KEY (CORRECT ANSWERS)

1.	A	11.	A
2.	C	12.	B
3.	A	13.	C
4.	C	14.	C
5.	C	15.	A
6.	C	16.	D
7.	A	17.	B
8.	C	18.	C
9.	A	19.	A
10.	A	20.	B

21.	D
22.	A
23.	A
24.	B
25.	A

TEST 2

DIRECTIONS: Each question or incomplete statement is followed by several suggested answers or completions. Select the one that BEST answers the question or completes the statement. *PRINT THE LETTER OF THE CORRECT ANSWER IN THE SPACE AT THE RIGHT.*

1. In analyzing data for the acquisition of new equipment, an analyst gathers the facts, analyzes them, and develops new procedures which will be required when the new equipment arrives.
Inn analyzing the factors involved, which one of the following is normally LEAST important in the evaluation of new equipment?
   A. Cost factors
   B. Layout and installation factors
   C. Production planning
   D. Operational experience of manufacturers of allied equipment

   1.____

2. If an analyst is required to recommend the selection of a machine for an office operation, he can BEST judge the expected output of a particular machine by pursuing which of the following courses of action?
Obtain
   A. an actual test run of the machine in his office
   B. data from the manufacturer of the machine
   C. information on the percentage of working time the machine will be used
   D. the experience of actual users of similar machines elsewhere

   2.____

3. Of the following, the BEST definition of records management is
   A. storage of all types of records at minimum expense
   B. planned control of all types of records
   C. storage of records for maximum accessibility
   D. systematic filing of all types of records

   3.____

4. The one of the following which is NOT a primary objective of a records retention and disposal system is to
   A. assure appropriate preservation of records having permanent value
   B. dispose of records not warranting further preservation
   C. establish retention standards for archives
   D. provide an opportunity to use miniaturization

   4.____

5. Of the following functions of management, the one which should NORMALLY precede the others is
   A. coordinating   B. directing   C. organizing   D. planning

   5.____

6. One of the more famous studies of organizations is called the Hawthorne study.
This work was one of the first to point out the importance of
   A. employee's benefit and retirement programs
   B. informal organization among employees
   C. job engineering
   D. styles of position classification

   6.____

7. In organization theory, the type of position in which an individual is appointed to give technical aid to management on a particular problem area is generally BEST termed a(n)
   A. administrative assistant
   B. assistant to
   C. staff assistant
   D. staff specialist

8. In organizing, doing what works in the particular situation, with due regard to both short- and long-range objective, is BEST termed
   A. ambivalence
   B. authoritarianism
   C. decentralization
   D. pragmatism

9. If an effort were made to reduce the number of private offices in a new layout, the LEAST effective substitute in offering privacy would be the use of
   A. an open area with lower movable partitions or railings separating each individual
   B. conference rooms
   C. larger desks
   D. modular desk units

10. The term *administrative substation* NORMALLY refers to
    A. a work station handling a number of office services for an office organization
    B. a work station where middle level supervisors are located
    C. an office for handling management trainees
    D. the functions allocated to particular levels of administrative managers

11. An operations research technique which would be applied to determine the optimum number of window clerks or interviewers to have in an agency serving the public would MOST likely be the use of
    A. line of balance
    B. queuing theory
    C. simulation
    D. work sampling

12. A type of file which permits the operator to remain seated while the file can be moved backward and forward as required is BEST termed a _____ file.
    A. lateral
    B. movable
    C. reciprocating
    D. rotary

13. The technique of work measurement in which the analyst observes the work at random times of the day is BEST termed
    A. indirect observation
    B. logging
    C. ratio delay
    D. wristwatch

14. Examples of predetermined time systems generally should include all of the following EXCEPT
    A. Master Clerical Data
    B. Methods Time Measurement
    C. Short Interval Data
    D. Work Factor

15. A technique by which the supervisor or an assistant distributes a predetermined batch of work to the employee at periodic intervals of the day is generally BEST known as 15.____
    A. backlog control scheduling
    B. production control scheduling
    C. short interval schedule
    D. workload balancing

16. E. Wright Bakke defined his *fusion process* as: The 16.____
    A. work environment to some degree remakes the organization and the organization to some degree remakes the work environment
    B. fusing of the interests of both management and labor unions
    C. community of interest between first line supervisors and top management
    D. organization to some degree remakes the individual and the individual to some degree remakes the organization

17. A pamphlet on issues related to 2020s-era office setup would likely be titled 17.____
    A. Close Encounters: How Proximity Elevates Production
    B. How Connectivity Spurs Inspiration
    C. See Your Employees in a New Light With Open Floor Plans
    D. From A to Zoom: The Terminology of the Hybrid Workplace

18. In planning office space for a newly established bureau, it would usually be LEAST desirable to 18.____
    A. concentrate, rather than disperse, the chief sources of office noises
    B. design an office environment with the same brightness as the office desk
    C. designate as reception rooms, washrooms, and other service areas those areas that will receive lesser amounts of illumination than those areas in which private office work will be performed
    D. eliminate natural light in cases where it is not the major light source

19. A private office should be used when its use is dictated by facts and unbiased judgment. It should never be provided simply because requests and sometimes pressure have been brought to bear. 19.____
    Of the following reasons used to justify use of a private office, the one that requires the MOST care in determining whether a private office is actually warranted is
    A. an office has always been provided for a particular job
    B. prestige considerations
    C. the confidential nature of the work
    D. the work involves high concentration

20. Theoretically, an ideal organization structure can be set up for each enterprise. In actual practice, the ideal organization structure is seldom, if ever, obtained. 20.____
    Of the following, the one that normally is of LEAST influence in determining the organization structure is the
    A. existence of agreements and favors among members of the organization
    B. funds available
    C. opinions and beliefs of top executives
    D. tendency of management to discard established forms in favor of new forms

21. An IMPORTANT aspect to keep in mind during the decision-making process is that
    A. all possible alternatives for attaining goals should be sought out and considered
    B. considering various alternatives only leads to confusion
    C. once a decision has been made, it cannot be retracted
    D. there is only one correct method to reach any goal

22. Implementation of accountability requires
    A. a leader who will not hesitate to take punitive action
    B. an established system of communication from the bottom to the top
    C. explicit directives from leaders
    D. too much expense to justify it

23. Of the following, the MAJOR difference between systems and procedures analysis and work simplification is:
    A. The former complicates organizational routine and the latter simplifies it
    B. The former is objective and the latter is subjective
    C. The former generally utilizes expert advice and the latter is a *do-it-yourself* improvement by supervisors and workers
    D. There is no difference other than in name

24. Systems development is concerned with providing
    A. a specific set of work procedures
    B. an overall framework to describe general relationships
    C. definitions of particular organizational functions
    D. organizational symbolism

25. Organizational systems and procedures should be
    A. developed as problems arise as no design can anticipate adequately the requirements of an organization
    B. developed jointly by experts in systems and procedures and the people who are responsible for implementing them
    C. developed solely by experts in systems and procedures
    D. eliminated whenever possible to save unnecessary expense

KEY (CORRECT ANSWERS)

1.	D	11.	B
2.	A	12.	C
3.	B	13.	C
4.	D	14.	C
5.	D	15.	C
6.	B	16.	D
7.	D	17.	D
8.	D	18.	D
9.	C	19.	A
10.	A	20.	D

21.	A
22.	B
23.	C
24.	B
25.	B

TEST 3

DIRECTIONS: Each question or incomplete statement is followed by several suggested answers or completions. Select the one that BEST answers the question or completes the statement. *PRINT THE LETTER OF THE CORRECT ANSWER IN THE SPACE AT THE RIGHT.*

1. The CHIEF danger of a decentralized control system is that
    A. excessive reports and communications will be generated
    B. problem areas may not be detected readily
    C. the expense will become routine
    D. this will result in too many *chiefs*

2. Of the following, management guides and controls clerical work PRINCIPALLY through
    A. close supervision and constant checking of personnel
    B. spot checking of clerical procedures
    C. strong sanctions for clerical supervisors
    D. the use of printed forms

3. Which of the following is MOST important before conducting fact-finding interviews?
    A. Becoming acquainted with all personnel to be interviewed
    B. Explaining the techniques you plan to use
    C. Explaining to the operating officials the purpose and scope of the study
    D. Orientation of the physical layout

4. Of the following, the one that is NOT essential in carrying out a comprehensive work improvement program is
    A. standards of performance
    B. supervisory training
    C. work count/task list
    D. work distribution chart

5. Which of the following control techniques is MOST useful on large complex systems projects?
    A. A general work plan
    B. Gantt chart
    C. Monthly progress report
    D. PERT chart

6. The action which is MOST effective in gaining acceptance of a study by the agency which is being studied is
    A. a directive from the agency head to install a study based on recommendations included in a report
    B. a lecture-type presentation following approval of the procedures
    C. a written procedure in narrative form covering the proposed system with visual presentations and discussions
    D. procedural charts showing the *before* situation, forms, steps, etc. to the employees affected

2 (#3)

7. Which of the following is NOT an advantage in the use of oral instructions as compared with written instructions? Oral instruction(s)
   A. can easily be changed
   B. is superior in transmitting complex directives
   C. facilitate exchange of information between a superior and his subordinate
   D. with discussions make it easier to ascertain understanding

7._____

8. Which organization principle is MOST closely related to procedural analysis and improvement?
   A. Duplication, overlapping, and conflict should be eliminated.
   B. Managerial authority should be clearly defined.
   C. The objectives of the organization should be clearly defined.
   D. Top management should be freed of burdensome detail.

8._____

9. Which one of the following is the MAJOR objective of operational audits?
   A. Detecting fraud
   B. Determining organization problems
   C. Determining the number of personnel needed
   D. Recommending opportunities for improving operating and management practices

9._____

10. Of the following, the formalization of organization structure is BEST achieved by
    A. a narrative description of the plan of organization
    B. functional charts
    C. job descriptions together with organization charts
    D. multi-flow charts

10._____

11. Budget planning is MOST useful when it achieves
    A. cost control   B. forecast of receipts
    C. performance review   D. personnel reduction

11._____

12. The UNDERLYING principle of sound administration is to
    A. base administration on investigation facts
    B. have plenty of resources available
    C. hire a strong administrator
    D. establish a broad policy

12._____

13. Although questionnaires are not the best survey tool the management analyst has to use, there are times when a good questionnaire can expedite the *fact-finding* phase of a management survey.
    Which of the following should be AVOIDED in the design and distribution of the questionnaire?
    A. Questions should be framed so that answers can be classified and tabulated for analysis.
    B. Those receiving the questionnaire must be knowledgeable enough to accurately provide the information desired.

13._____

52

C. The questionnaire should enable the respondent to answer in a narrative manner.
D. The questionnaire should require a minimum amount of writing.

14. Of the following, the formula which is used to calculate the arithmetic mean from data grouped in a frequency distribution is M =

    A. $\dfrac{N}{\Sigma fx}$ B. $N(\Sigma fx)$ C. $\dfrac{\Sigma fx}{N}$ D. $\dfrac{\Sigma x}{fN}$

15. Arranging large groups of numbers in frequency distributions
    A. gives a more composite picture of the total group than a random listing
    B. is misleading in most cases
    C. is unnecessary in most instances
    D. presents the data in a form whereby further manipulation of the group is eliminated

16. After a budget has been developed, it serves to
    A. assist the accounting department in posting expenditures
    B. measure the effectiveness of department managers
    C. provide a yardstick against which actual costs are measured
    D. provide the operating department with total expenditure to date

17. Of the following, which formula is used to determine staffing requirements?

    A. $\dfrac{\text{Hours per man-day}}{\text{Volume x Standard}}$ = Employees Needed

    B. $\dfrac{\text{Hours per man-day x Standard}}{\text{Volume}}$ = Employees Needed

    C. $\dfrac{\text{Hours per man-day x Volume}}{\text{Standard}}$ = Employees Needed

    D. $\dfrac{\text{Volume x Standard}}{\text{Hours per man-day}}$ = Employees Needed

18. Of the following, which formula is used to determine the number of days required to process work?

    A. $\dfrac{\text{Employees x Daily Output}}{\text{Volume}}$ = Days to Process Work

    B. $\dfrac{\text{Employees x Volume}}{\text{Daily Output}}$ = Days to Process Work

    C. $\dfrac{\text{Volume}}{\text{Employees x Daily Output}}$ = Days to Process Work

    D. $\dfrac{\text{Volume x Daily Output}}{\text{Employees}}$ = Days to Process Work

19. Identify this symbol, as used in a Systems Flow Chart. 19.____
    A. Document
    B. Decision
    C. Preparation
    D. Process

20. Of the following, the MAIN advantage of a form letter over a dictated letter is that a form letter 20.____
    A. is more expressive
    B. is neater
    C. may be mailed in a window envelope
    D. requires less secretarial time

21. The term that may be defined as a *systematic analysis of all factors affecting work being done or all factors that will affect work to be done, in order to save effort, time, or money* is 21.____
    A. flow process charting
    B. work flow analysis
    C. work measurement
    D. work simplification

22. Generally, the LEAST important basic factor to be considered in developing office layout improvements is to locate 22.____
    A. office equipment, reference facilities, and files as close as practicable to those using them
    B. persons as close as practicable to the persons from whom they receive their work
    C. persons as close as practicable to windows and/or adequate ventilation
    D. persons who are friendly with each other close together to improve morale

23. Of the following, the one which is LEAST effective in reducing administrative costs is 23.____
    A. applying objective measurement techniques to determine the time required to perform a given task
    B. establishing budgets on the basis of historical performance data
    C. motivating supervisors and managers in the importance of cost reduction
    D. selecting the best method—manual, mechanical, or electronic—to process the essential work

24. *Fire-fighting* is a common expression in management terminology. 24.____
    Of the following, which BEST describes *fire-fighting* as an analyst's approach to solving paperwork problems?
    A. A complete review of all phases of the department's processing functions
    B. A studied determination of the proper equipment to process the work
    C. An analysis of each form that is being processed and the logical reasons for its processing
    D. The solution of problems as they arise, usually at the request of operating personnel

25. Assume that an analyst with a proven record of accomplishment on many projects is having difficulties on his present assignment.
 Of the following, the BEST course of action for his superior to take is to
 A. assume there is a personality conflict involved and transfer the analyst to another project
 B. give the analyst some time off
 C. review the nature of the project to determine whether or not the analyst is equipped to handle the assignment
 D. suggest that the analyst seek counseling

KEY (CORRECT ANSWERS)

1. B
2. D
3. C
4. B
5. D

6. C
7. B
8. A
9. D
10. C

11. A
12. A
13. C
14. C
15. A

16. C
17. D
18. C
19. A
20. D

21. D
22. D
23. B
24. D
25. C

EXAMINATION SECTION
TEST 1

DIRECTIONS: Each question or incomplete statement is followed by several suggested answers or completions. Select the one that BEST answers the question or completes the statement. *PRINT THE LETTER OF THE CORRECT ANSWER IN THE SPACE AT THE RIGHT.*

1. With a management staff of 15 capable analysts, which of the following organizational approaches would generally be BEST for overall results? Organization
    A. by specialists in fields, such as management, organization, systems analysis
    B. by clientele to be served, such as hospitals, police education, social services
    C. where all 15 report directly to head of the management staff
    D. by specialized study groups with flexibility in assigning staff under a qualified project leader

2. In conducting a general management survey to identify problems and opportunities, which of the following would it be LEAST necessary to consider?
    A. Identifying program and planning deficiencies in each functional area
    B. Organization problems
    C. Sound management practices not being used
    D. The qualifications of the supervisory personnel

3. Which of the following statements MOST accurately defines *operations research*?
    A. A highly sophisticated system used in the analysis of management problems
    B. A specialized application of electronic data processing in the analysis of management problems
    C. Research on operating problems
    D. The application of sophisticated mathematical tools to the analysis of management problems

4. Theoretically, an ideal organization structure can be set up for each enterprise. In actual practice, the ideal organization structure is seldom, if ever, obtained. Of the following, the one that is of LEAST influence in determining the organization structure is the
    A. existence of agreements and favors among members of the organization
    B. funds available
    C. growing trend of management to discard established forms in favor of new forms
    D. opinions and beliefs of top executives

5. To which one of the following is it MOST important that the functional or technical staff specialist in a large organization devote major attention?
   A. Conducting audits of line operations
   B. Controlling of people in the line organization
   C. Developing improve approaches, plans, and procedures and assisting the line organization in their implementation
   D. Providing advice to his superior and to operating units

6. In the planning for reorganization of a department, which one of the following principles relating to the assignment of functions is NOT correct?
   A. Line and staff functions should be separated.
   B. Separate functions should be assigned to separate organizational units.
   C. There should be no disturbance of the previously assigned tasks of personnel.
   D. There should generally be no overlapping among organizational elements.

7. Results are BEST accomplished within an organization when the budgets and plans are developed by the
   A. budget office, independent of the operating units
   B. head of the operating unit based on analysis of prior year's operations after discussion with his superior
   C. head of the operating unit with general guidelines and data from higher authority and the budget office, and input from key personnel
   D. head of the organization unit based on an analysis of prior year's operations

8. The *management process* is a term used to describe the responsibilities common to
   A. all levels of management
   B. first-line supervisors
   C. middle management jobs
   D. top management jobs

9. Of the following, committees are BEST used for
   A. advising the head of the organization
   B. improving functional work
   C. making executive decisions
   D. making specific planning decisions

10. Which of the following would NOT be a part of a management control system?
    A. An objective test of new ideas or methods in operation
    B. Determination of need for organization improvement
    C. Objective comparison of operating results
    D. Provision of information useful for revising objectives, programs, and operations

11. Of the following, the one which a line role generally does NOT include is   11.____
    A. controlling results and performance
    B. coordination work and exchanging ideas with other line organizations
    C. implementation of approved plans developed by staff
    D. planning work and making operation decisions

12. In a normal curve, one standard deviation would include MOST NEARLY what   12.____
    percentage of the cases involved?
    A. 50%   B. 68%   C. 95%   D. 99%

13. The Office Layout Chart is a sketch of the physical arrangements of the office   13.____
    to which has been added the flow lines of the principal work performed there.
    Which one of the following states the BEST advantage of superimposing the
    work flow onto the desk layout?
    A. Lighting and acoustics can be improved.
    B. Line and staff relationships can be determined.
    C. Obvious misarrangements can be corrected.
    D. The number of delays can be determined.

14. An advantage of the Multiple Process Chart over the Flow Process Chart is that   14.____
    the Multiple Process Chart shows the
    A. individual worker's activity
    B. number of delays
    C. sequence of operations
    D. simultaneous flow of work in several departments

15. Of the following, which is the MAJOR advantage of a microfilm record retention   15.____
    system?
    A. Filing can follow the terminal digit system.
    B. Retrieving documents from the files is faster.
    C. Significant space is saved in storing records.
    D. To read a microfilm record, a film reader is not necessary.

16. Which one of the following questions should the management analyst generally   16.____
    consider FIRST?
    A. How is it being done? and Why should it be done that way?
    B. What is being done? and Why is it necessary?
    C. When should this job be done? and What should he do it?
    D. Who should do the job? and Why should he do it?

17. Assume that you are in the process of eliminating unnecessary forms.   17.____
    The answer to which one of the following questions would be LEAST relevant?
    A. Could the information be obtained elsewhere?
    B. Is the form properly designed?
    C. Is the form used as intended?
    D. Is the purpose of the form essential to the operation?

18. Use of color in forms adds to their cost. Sometimes, however, the use of color will greatly simplify procedure and more than pay for itself in time saved and errors eliminated.
    This is ESPECIALLY true when
    A. a form passes through many reviewers
    B. considerable sorting is required
    C. the form is other than a standard size
    D. the form will not be sent through the mail

18.____

19. Of the following techniques, the one GENERALLY employed and considered BEST in forms design is to divide writing lines into boxes with captions printed in small type _____ of the box.
    A. centered in the lower part
    B. centered in the upper part
    C. in the upper left-hand corner
    D. in the lower right-hand corner

19.____

20. Many forms authorities advocate the construction of a functional forms file or index.
    If such a file is set up, the MOST effective way of classifying forms for such an index is classification by
    A. department
    B. form number
    C. name or type of form
    D. subject to which the form applies

20.____

21. An interrelated pattern of jobs which makes up the structure of a system is known as
    A. a chain of command
    B. cybernetics
    C. the formal organization
    D. the maintenance pattern

21.____

22. A transparent sheet of film containing multiple rows of microimages is characteristic of which one of the following types of microfilm?
    A. Aperture
    B. Jacket
    C. Microfiche
    D. Roll or reel

22.____

23. PRIMARY responsibility for training and development of employees generally rests with
    A. outside training agencies
    B. the individual who needs training
    C. the line supervisor
    D. the training specialist in the Personnel Office

23.____

24. Which of the following approaches usually provides the BEST communication in the objectives and values of a new program which is to be introduced?
    A. A general written description of the program by the program manager for review by those who share responsibility
    B. An effective verbal presentation by the program manager to those affected
    C. Development of the plan and operational approach in carrying out the program by the program manager assisted by his key subordinates
    D Development of the plan by the program manager's supervisor

24.____

25. The term *total systems concept*, as used in electronic data processing, refers
    A. only to the computer and its associated electronic accessories
    B. only o the paper information output, or *software* aspect
    C. to a large computer-based information handling system, which supplies the information needs of an entire agency or corporation
    D. to all of the automated and manual information systems in a specific subdivision of an organization

26. Of the following, scientific management can BEST be considered as an attempt to establish work procedures
    A. in fields of scientific endeavors
    B. which are beneficial only to bosses
    C. which require less control
    D. utilizing the concept of a man-machine system

27. The MAJOR failing of efficiency engineering was that it
    A. overlooked the human factor
    B. required experts to implement the techniques
    C. was not based on true scientific principles
    D. was too costly and time consuming

28. Which of the following organizations is MOST noted throughout the world for its training in management?
    A. American Management Association
    B. American Political Science Association
    C. Society for the Advancement of Management
    D. Systems and Procedures Association

29. The GENERAL method of arriving at program objectives should be
    A. a trial and error process
    B. developed as the program progresses
    C. included in the program plan
    D. left to the discretion of the immediate supervisors

30. The review and appraisal of an organization to determine waste and deficiencies, improved methods, better means of control, more efficient operations, and greater use of human and physical facilities is known as a(n)
    A. management audit   B. manpower survey
    C. work simplification   D. operations audit

31. When data are grouped into a frequency distribution, the *median* is BEST defined as the _____ in the distribution.
    A. 50% point   B. largest single range
    C. smallest single range   D. point of greatest concentration

32. The manual, visual, and mental elements into which an operation may be analyzed in time and motion study are denoted by the term
    A. measurement   B. positioning   C. standards   D. therbligs

33. Of the following, the symbol shown at the right, as used in a systems flow chart, denotes
    A. decision
    B. document
    C. manual operation
    D. process

33.____

34. Of the following agencies of city government, the one with the LARGEST expense budget for the current fiscal year is the
    A. environmental protection administration
    B. department of social services
    C. municipal service administration
    D. police department

34.____

35. A feasibility study is the first phase in the process of conversion from manual to computerized data processing.
    The phases, in sequence, are the feasibility study, system
    A. conversion, system installation, follow up
    B. design, installation
    C. design, follow up, installation
    D. design, system conversion, installation

35.____

36.

    The type of chart illustrated above is generally known as a _____ Chart.
    A. Flow   B. Gantt
    C. Work Simplification   D. Motion-Time Study

36.____

37.

37.____

The type of chart illustrated on the previous page is generally known as a _____ Chart.
   A. Flow
   B. Gantt
   C. Simo
   D. Work Simplification

38.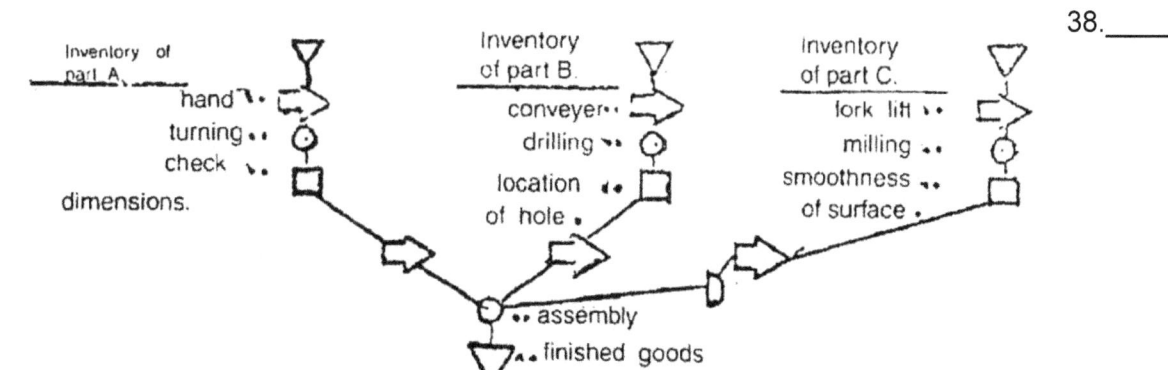

The type of chart illustrated above is generally known as a(n) _____ Chart.
   A. Multiple Activity
   B. Motion-Time
   C. Work Place Layout
   D. Operation Process

39.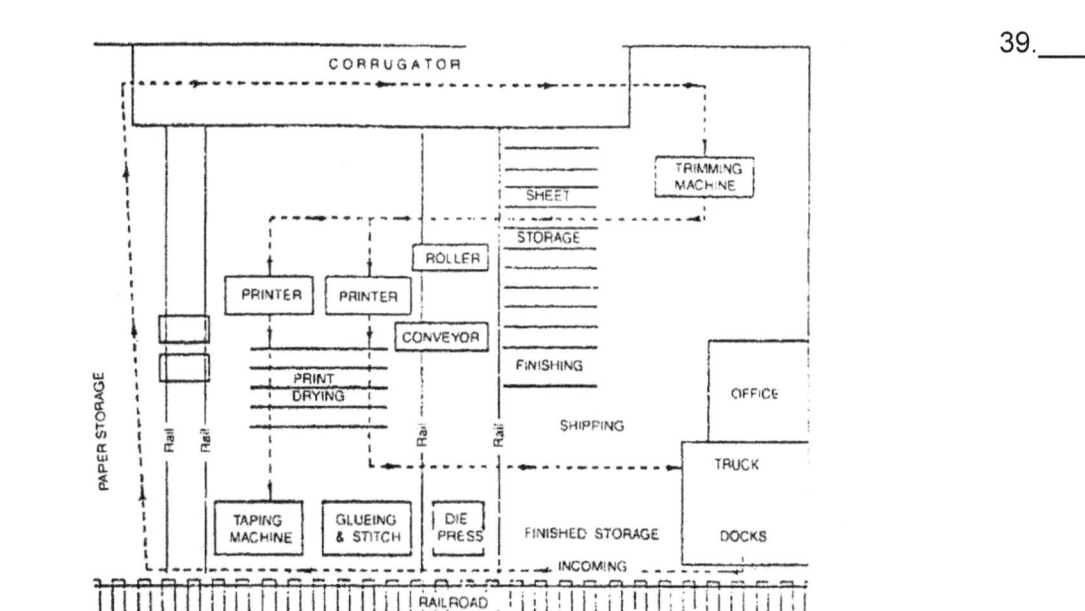

The one illustrated above is generally known as a
   A. Gantt Chart
   B. Multiple Activity Chart
   C. Planned Flow Diagram
   D. Work Place Diagram

40.

The type of chart illustrated above is generally known as a(n) _____ Chart.
A. Analysis
B. Flow Process
C. Man or Material
D. Multiple Activity

KEY (CORRECT ANSWERS)

1.	D	11.	B	21.	C	31.	A
2.	D	12.	B	22.	C	32.	D
3.	D	13.	C	23.	C	33.	A
4.	C	14.	D	24.	C	34.	B
5.	C	15.	C	25.	C	35.	D
6.	C	16.	B	26.	D	36.	B
7.	C	17.	B	27.	A	37.	C
8.	A	18.	B	28.	A	38.	D
9.	A	19.	C	29.	C	39.	C
10.	B	20.	D	30.	A	40.	B

TEST 2

DIRECTIONS: Each question or incomplete statement is followed by several suggested answers or completions. Select the one that BEST answers the question or completes the statement. *PRINT THE LETTER OF THE CORRECT ANSWER IN THE SPACE AT THE RIGHT.*

1. The one of the following which is MOST important in getting a systems survey off to a good start is
   A. a kick-off meeting with key personnel covering the purpose of the study and introduction of the survey staff
   B. a prior knowledge of the organization manual, charts, and statement of responsibility
   C. knowledge of personality problems in the agency needing special attention
   D. written announcement from the agency head

2. Which of the following is the LEAST important factor in planning an administrative survey?
   A. Developing a work plan and time schedule
   B. Knowledge of sound organization concepts and principles
   C. Survey techniques and methods to be used for analysis in compiling data needed
   D. The purpose, scope, and level of the survey

3. Assume that a supervisor, when reviewing a decision reached by one of his subordinates, finds the decision incorrect.
   Under these circumstances, it would be MOST desirable for the supervisor to
   A. correct the decision and inform the subordinate of this at a staff meeting
   B. correct the decision and suggest a more detailed analysis in the future
   C. help the employee find the reason for the correct decision
   D. refrain from assigning this type of problem to the employee

4. After an analyst has identified a problem area, which one of the following is the MOST important step in getting management to recognize that a problem does exist?
   A. A brief statement describing the problem
   B. Implications if problem is not corrected
   C. Relationship to other problems
   D. Supporting factual evidence and data indicating that the problem does exist

5. The statement, *work expands to fit the time available for its completion*, refers MOST directly to
   A. job enlargement principles   B. Parkinson's Law
   C. The Open System Theory   D. The Peter Principle

6. A comprehensive and constructive examination of a company, institution, or branch of government, or of any of its components such as an agency, division, or department, and its plans and objectives, methods of control, its means of operations, and its use of human and physical facilities is COMMONLY known as a(n) _____ audit.
   A. systems
   B. extensive financial
   C. operational or management
   D. organizational

6.____

7. Assume you are assigned to analyze the details of the procedures a clerk follows in order to complete filling out an invoice or a requisition. Your purpose is to simplify and shorten the procedure he has been trained to use.
The MOST appropriate chart for this purpose would be the
   A. block flow diagram
   B. flow process chart
   C. forms flow chart
   D. work distribution chart

7.____

8. In identifying problems and opportunities for improvement, which one of the following is MOST closely related to organization planning?
   A. Effective operating procedures issued from headquarters
   B. Effective records management
   C. Need for improved management concepts and practices
   D. Review of the salary and wage administration program

8.____

9. MOST of the working time of the functional or technical staff specialist in a large organization should be focused on
   A. conducting audits of line operations
   B. developing improved approaches, plans, and procedures and assisting the line organization in their implementation
   C. providing advice to his superior and to operating units
   D. the number of people in the line organization

9.____

10. The LEAST effective way for a survey group to plan is to
    A. clarify objectives and identify problems
    B. conduct planning and review sessions annually when budgets are prepared
    C. periodically conduct review sessions for purposes of coordination
    D. undertake specific action programs

10.____

11. Which one of the following is the MOST important element of a good manpower plan?
    A. Establishing inventories of capable personnel
    B. Forecasting the number of people needed in the future
    C. Having the right people for all jobs when needed
    D. Identifying training needs

11.____

12. Completed staff work is MOST effective in accomplishing which one of the following?
    A. Determination of the problems of the line organization
    B. Determination of the staffing needs of an organization

12.____

C. Preparation of effective proposals and approaches to improve fine results
D. Review of budgets proposed by line organization

13. What generally is the PRINCIPAL objection to the use of form letters?
The
    A. difficulty of developing a form letter to serve the purpose
    B. excessive time involved in selecting the proper form letter
    C. errors in selecting form letters
    D. impersonality of form letters

14. What is the BEST approach for introducing change?
A
    A. combination of written and also verbal communication to all personnel affected by the change
    B. general bulletin to all personnel
    C. meeting pointing out all the values of the new approach
    D. written directive to key personnel

15. The FIRST step in designing an effective management survey is
    A. examining backlogs
    B. flow charting
    C. motion analysis and time study
    D. project planning

16. In statistical sampling, the error which will NOT be exceeded by 50 percent of the cases is known as the
    A. difference between two means
    B. probable error
    C. standard deviation
    D. standard error of the mean

17. In a normal or bell-shaped curve, the area encompassed by two standard deviations from the mean is
    A. 68%   B. 95%   C. 97%   D. 99%

18. The statistical average referring to that point on the scale at which the concentration is greatest or that value which occurs the greatest number of times and which might be taken as typical of the entire distribution is called the
    A. mean   B. median   C. mode   D. quartile

19. In process charting, the symbol which is used when conditions (except those which intentionally change the physical or chemical characteristics of the object) do not permit or require immediate performance is
    A. □   B. ○   C. D   D. ▽

20. Assume that you are making a study of a central headquarters office which processes claims received from a number of district offices. You notice the following problems: Some employees are usually busy, while others doing the same kind of work in the same grade have little to do, high level professional people frequently spend considerable time searching for files in the file room.

Which of the following charts would be MOST useful to record and analyze the data needed to help solve these problems?
_____ Chart.
- A. Forms Distribution
- B. Process
- C. Space Layout
- D. Work Distribution

21. Which of the following types of work would NOT be readily measured by conventional time study techniques?
Work
- A. of sufficient volume, uniform in nature, that will justify the cost of continuing and maintaining controls
- B. that is countable in precise quantitative terms
- C. that is essentially creative and considerably varied in content
- D. that is repetitive, uniform, and homogeneous in content over a period of time

21.____

22. Which of the following should be the FIRST consideration in a work simplification study?
Can the
- A. sequence be changed for improvement?
- B. task be combined with another?
- C. task be eliminated
- D. task be simplified?

22.____

23. In evaluating the sequence of operations involved in the clerical processing, which of the items listed below would be an indicator that methods improvements are needed?
- A. Some operations duplicate previous operations.
- B. The supervisor believes many of the company's policies are wrong.
- C. There is a high turnover of mail clerks.
- D. Work is logged into and out of the department.

23.____

24. Of the following, the one that is MOST likely to make a methods change unacceptable is when the
- A. change does not threaten the workers' security
- B. change follows a series of previously unsuccessful similar changes
- C. change has been well thought out and properly introduced
- D. people affected by the change have participated in the development of the changes

24.____

25. Which of the following questions has the LEAST significant bearing on the analysis of the paperwork flow?
- A. How is the work brought into the department and how is it taken away?
- B. How many workstations are involved in processing the work within the department?
- C. Is the work received and removed in the proper quantity?
- D. Where is the supervisor's desk located in relationship to those he supervises?

25.____

26. Which of the following does NOT have significant bearing on the arrangement, sequence, and zoning of information into box captions?
The
    A. layout of the source documents from which the information is taken
    B. logical flow of data
    C. needs of forms to be prepared from this form
    D. type of print to be employed

27. In determining the spacing requirements of a form and the size of the boxes to be used, PRIMARY consideration should be given to the
    A. distribution of the form
    B. method of entry, i.e., handwritten or machine and type of machine
    C. number of copies
    D. number of items to be entered

28. Of the following, the BEST technique to follow when providing instructions for the completion and routing of a form is to _____ the form.
    A. imprint the instructions on the face of
    B. imprint the instructions on the back of
    C. provide a written procedure to accompany
    D. provide verbal instructions when issuing

29. A forms layout style where a separate space in the shape of a box is provided for each item of information requested and the caption or question for each item is shown in the upper left-hand corner of each box is known as the _____ style.
    A. box
    B. checkbox
    C. checklist
    D. checkbox and checklist

30. It is the office manager's responsibility to promote office safety and eliminate hazards. A number of policies and procedures are widely advocated and followed by management and safety experts.
    Of the following, the policy or procedure that is LEAST valid is:
    A. Each department supervisor should be required to complete a report at the time of each accident so that the person in charge of safety administration will be able to analyze the pattern of common causes and improve safety conditions.
    B. Electrical cords and connectors for machines and equipment should be routinely checked so as to eliminate fire and shock hazards.
    C. Employees should be informed of the type of accidents which may occur
    D. Smoking at desks should be prohibited so as to avoid the possibility of fire hazards; and a lounge provided for this purpose.

31. An effective discussion leader is one who
    A. announces the problem and his preconceived solution at the start of the discussion
    B. guides and directs the discussion according to pre-arranged outline
    C. interrupts or corrects confused participants to save time
    D. permits anyone to say anything at anytime

32. Under what circumstances would it be MOST advisable to have two or more clerks in a department share the same adding machine?
    When
    A. capital appropriations are tight
    B. the clerks sharing the adding machine are located at adjacent desks
    C. the clerks sharing the adding machine get along with one another
    D. the need for the equipment is so little that there is negligible time lost in sharing the adding machine

33. Of the following, the statement that is MOST descriptive of, and fundamental to, proper office landscaping is:
    A. All clerical desks should be arranged singly and in rows
    B. The layout should be built around the flow of information and work in the office.
    C. The layout should be built around the recognized organizational hierarchy of the office unit.
    D. There should be many planters arranged to give the office an open look.

34. The MOST significant factor to be considered in deciding on upgrades to clerical-related software is
    A. reduction of costs
    B. standardization of software across all departments
    C. availability of new and innovative features
    D. compatibility and efficiency related to clerical tasks

35. The human relations movement in management theory is BASICALLY concerned with
    A. counteracting employee unrest
    B. eliminating the *time and motion* man
    C. interrelationships among individuals in organizations
    D. the psychology of the worker

36. PERT, as commonly used, stood for
    A. Periodic Estimate of Resource Trends
    B. Potential Energy Research Technology
    C. Professional Engineer Review Tests
    D. Program Evaluation and Review Technique

37. The BEST type of chart to use in showing the absolute movement or change of a continuous series of data over a period of time, such as changes in prices, employment, or expenses, is usually a _____ chart.
    A. bar   B. line   C. multiple bar   D. pie

38. Software designed for statistical record keeping and organization is called
    A. Navigator   B. Acrobat   C. Outlook   D. Excel

39. Due to its size, a tablet (ex. iPad) has ____ than a standard office computer.   39.____
    A. less reliability   B. less computing power
    C. more functionality   D. none of the above

40. Of the following, the one theme that has NOT had an elevated impact on   40.____
    computing and business in the 2020s is
    A. free unlimited access to email
    B. advanced mobile technology
    C. developments in artificial intelligence (AI)
    D. automation of service tasks

KEY (CORRECT ANSWERS)

1.	A	11.	C	21.	C	31.	B
2.	B	12.	C	22.	C	32.	D
3.	C	13.	D	23.	A	33.	B
4.	D	14.	A	24.	B	34.	D
5.	B	15.	D	25.	D	35.	C
6.	C	16.	B	26.	D	36.	D
7.	B	17.	B	27.	B	37.	B
8.	C	18.	C	28.	A	38.	D
9.	B	19.	C	29.	A	39.	D
10.	B	20.	D	30.	D	40.	A

READING COMPREHENSION
UNDERSTANDING AND INTERPRETING WRITTEN MATERIAL
EXAMINATION SECTION

This exam section includes some passages and questions related to functions of the first computerized offices, which consisted of typewriters and other such manual office equipment.

TEST 1

DIRECTIONS: Each question or incomplete statement is followed by several suggested answers or completions. Select the one that BEST answers the question or completes the statement. *PRINT THE LETTER OF THE CORRECT ANSWER IN THE SPACE AT THE RIGHT.*

Questions 1-2.

DIRECTIONS: Questions 1 and 2 are to be answered SOLELY on the basis of the following passage.

The employees in a unit or division of a government agency may be referred to as a work group. Within a government agency which has existed for some time, the work groups will have evolved traditions of their own. The persons in these work groups acquire these traditions as part of the process of work adjustment within their groups. Usually, a work group in a large organization will contain *oldtimers*, *newcomers*, and *in-betweeners*. Like the supervisor of a group, who is not necessarily an oldtimer or the oldest member, oldtimers usually have great influence. They can recall events unknown to others and are a storehouse of information and advice about current problems in the light of past experience. They pass along the traditions of the group to the others who, in turn, become oldtimers themselves. Thus, the traditions of the group which have been honored and revered by long acceptance are continued.

1. According to the above passage, the traditions of a work group within a government agency are developed
    A. at the time the group is established
    B. over a considerable period of time
    C. in order to give recognition to oldtimers
    D. for the group before it is established

2. According to the above passage, the oldtimers within a work group
    A. are the means by which long accepted practices and customs are perpetuated
    B. would best be able to settle current problems that arise
    C. are honored because of the changes they have made in the traditions
    D. have demonstrated that they have learned to do their work well

Questions 3-4.

DIRECTIONS: Questions 3 and 4 are to be answered SOLELY on the following passage.

In public agencies, the success of a person assigned to perform first-line supervisory duties depends in large part upon the personal relations between him and his subordinate employees. The goal of supervising effort is something more than to obtain compliance with procedures established by some central office. The major objective is work accomplishment. In order for this goal to be attained, employees must want to attain it and must exercise initiative in their work. Only if employees are generally satisfied with the type of supervision which exists in an organization will they put forth their best efforts.

3. According to the above passage, in order for employees to try to do their work as well as they can, it is essential that
   A. they participate in determining their working conditions and rates of pay
   B. their supervisors support the employees' viewpoints in meetings with higher management
   C. they are content with the supervisory practices which are being used
   D. their supervisors make the changes in working procedures that the employees request

3.____

4. It can be inferred from the above passage that the goals of a unit in a public agency will not be reached unless the employees in the unit
   A. wish to reach them and are given the opportunity to make individual contributions to the work
   B. understand the relationship between the goals of the unit and goals of the agency
   C. have satisfactory personal relationships with employees of other units in the agency
   D. carefully follow the directions issued by higher authorities

4.____

Questions 5-9.

DIRECTIONS: Questions 5 through 9 are to be answered SOLELY on the basis of the following passage.

In an employee thinks he can save money, time, or material for the city or has an idea about how to do something better than it is being done, he shouldn't keep it to himself. He should send his ideas to the Employees' Suggestion Program, using the special form which is kept on hand in all departments. An employee may send in as many ideas as he wishes. To make sure that each idea is judged fairly, the name of the suggester is not made known until an award is made. The awards are certificate of merit or cash prizes ranging from $10 to $500.

5. According to the above passage, an employee who knows how to do a job in a better way should
   A. be sure it saves enough time to be worthwhile
   B. get paid the money he saves for the city
   C. keep it to himself to avoid being accused of causing a speed-up
   D. send his idea to the Employees' Suggestion Program

5.____

6. In order to send his idea to the Employees' Suggestion Program, an employee should
    A. ask the Department of Personnel for a special form
    B. get the special form in his own department
    C. mail the idea using Special Delivery
    D. send it on plain, white letter-size paper

7. An employee may send to the Employees' Suggestion Program
    A. as many ideas as he can think of
    B. no more than one idea each week
    C. no more than ten ideas in a month
    D. only one idea on each part of the job

8. The reason the name of an employee who makes a suggestion is not made known at first is to
    A. give the employee a larger award
    B. help the judges give more awards
    C. insure fairness in judging
    D. only one idea on each part of the job

9. An employee whose suggestion receives an award may be given a
    A. bonus once a year
    B. certificate for $10
    C. cash prize of up to $500
    D. salary increase of $500

Questions 10-12.

DIRECTIONS: Questions 10 through 12 are to be answered SOLELY on the basis of the following passage.

According to the rules of the Department of Personnel, the work of every permanent city employee is reviewed and rated by his supervisor at least once a year. The civil service rating system gives the employee and his supervisor a chance to talk about the progress made during the past year as well as about those parts of the job in which the employee needs to do better. In order to receive a pay increase each year, the employee must have a satisfactory service rating. Service ratings also count toward an employee's final mark on a promotion examination.

10. According to the above passage, a permanent city employee is rated AT LEAST once
    A. before his work is reviewed
    B. every six months
    C. yearly by his supervisor
    D. yearly by the Department of Personnel

11. According to the above passage, under the rating system the supervisor and the employee can discuss how
    A. much more work needs to be done next year
    B. the employee did his work last year
    C. the work can be made easier next year
    D. the work of the Department can be increased

12. According to the above passage, a permanent city employee will NOT receive a yearly pay increase
    A. if he received a pay increase the year before
    B. if he used his service rating for his mark on a promotion examination
    C. if his service rating is unsatisfactory
    D. unless he got some kind of a service rating

Questions 13-16.

DIRECTIONS: Questions 13 through 16 are to be answered SOLELY on the basis of the following passage.

It is an accepted fact that the rank and file employee can frequently advance worthwhile suggestions toward increasing efficiency. For this reason, an Employees' Suggestion System has been developed and put into operation. Suitable means have been provided at each departmental location for the confidential submission of suggestions. Numerous suggestions have been received thus far and, after study, about five percent of the ideas submitted are being translated into action. It is planned to set up, eventually, monetary awards for all worthwhile suggestions.

13. According to the above passage, a MAJOR reason why an Employees' Suggestion System was established is that
    A. an organized program of improvement is better than a haphazard one
    B. employees can often give good suggestions to increase efficiency
    C. once a fact is accepted, it is better to act on it than to do nothing
    D. the suggestions of rank and file employees were being neglected

14. According to the above passage, under the Employees' Suggestion System,
    A. a file of worthwhile suggestions will eventually be set up at each departmental location
    B. it is possible for employees to turn in suggestions without fellow employees knowing of it
    C. means have been provided for the regular and frequent collection of suggestions submitted
    D. provision has been made for the judging of worthwhile suggestions by an Employees' Suggestion Committee

15. According to the above passage, it is reasonable to assume that
    A. all suggestions must be turned in at a central office
    B. employees who make worthwhile suggestions will be promoted
    C. not all the prizes offered will be monetary ones
    D. prizes of money will be given for the best suggestions

16. According to the above passage, of the many suggestions made,
    A. all are first tested
    B. a small part are put into use
    C. most are very worthwhile
    D. samples are studied

5 (#1)

Questions 17-20.

DIRECTIONS: Questions 17 through 20 are to be answered SOLELY on the basis of the following passage.

Employees may be granted leaves of absence without pay at the discretion of the Personnel Officer. Such a leave without pay shall begin on the first working day on which the employee does not report for duty and shall continue to the first day on which the employee returns to duty. The Personnel Division may vary the dates of the leave for the record so as to conform with payroll periods, but in no case shall an employee be off the payroll for a different number of calendar days than would have been the case if the actual dates mentioned above had been used. An employee who has vacation or overtime to his credit, which is available for normal use, may take time off immediately prior to beginning a leave of absence without pay, chargeable against all or part of such vacation or overtime.

17. According to the above passage, the Personnel Officer must   17.____
    A. decide if a leave of absence without pay should be granted
    B. require that a leave end on the last working day of a payroll period
    C. see to it that a leave of absence to conform with a payroll period
    D. vary the dates of a leave of absence to conform with a payroll period

18. According to the above passage, the exact dates of a leave of absence without   18.____
    pay may be varied provided that the
    A. calendar days an employee is off the payroll equal the actual leave granted
    B. leave conforms to an even number of payroll periods
    C. leave when granted made provision for variance to simplify payroll records
    D. Personnel Officer approves the variation

19. According to the above passage, a leave of absence without pay must extend   19.____
    from the
    A. first day of a calendar period to the first day the employee resumes work
    B. first day of a payroll period to the last calendar day of the leave
    C. first working day missed to the first day on which the employee resumes work
    D. last day on which an employee works through the first day he returns to work

20. According to the above passage, an employee may take extra time off just   20.____
    before the start of a leave of absence without pay if
    A. he charges this extra time against his leave
    B. he has a favorable balance of vacation or overtime which has been frozen
    C. the vacation or overtime that he would normally use for a leave without pay has not been charged in this way before
    D. there is time to his credit which he may use

Question 21.

DIRECTIONS: Question 21 is to be answered SOLELY on the basis of the following passage.

In considering those things which are motivators and incentives to work, it might be just as erroneous not to give sufficient weight to money as an incentive as it is to give too much weight. It is not a problem of establishing a rank-order of importance, but one of knowing that motivation is a blend or mixture rather than a pure element. It is simple to say that cultural factors count more than financial considerations, but this leads only to the conclusion that our society is financial-oriented.

21. Based on the above passage, in our society, cultural and social motivations to work are
    A. things which cannot be avoided
    B. melded to financial incentives
    C. of less consideration than high pay
    D. not balanced equally with economic or financial considerations

21.____

Question 22.

DIRECTIONS: Question 22 is to be answered SOLELY on the basis of the following passage.

A general principle of training and learning with respect to people is that they learn more readily if they receive *feedback*. Essential to maintaining proper motivational levels is knowledge of results which indicate level of progress. Feedback also assists the learning process by identifying mistakes. If this kind of information were not given to the learner, then improper or inappropriate job performance may be instilled.

22. Based on the above passage, which of the following is MOST accurate?
    A. Learning will not take place without feedback.
    B. In the absence of feedback, improper or inappropriate job performance will be learned.
    C. To properly motivate a learner, the learner must have his progress made known to him.
    D. Trainees should be told exactly what to do if they are to learn properly

22.____

Questions 23.

DIRECTIONS: Question 23 is to be answered SOLELY on the basis of the following passage.

In a democracy, the obligation of public officials is twofold. They must not only do an efficient and satisfactory job of administration, but also they must persuade the public that it is an efficient and satisfactory job. It is a burden which, if properly assumed, will make democracy work and perpetuate reform government.

23. The above passage means that
    A. public officials should try to please everybody

23.____

B. public opinion is instrumental if determining the policy of public officials
C. satisfactory performance of the job of administration will eliminate opposition to its work
D. frank and open procedure in a public agency will aid in maintaining progressive government

Question 24.

DIRECTIONS: Question 24 is to be answered SOLELY on the basis of the following passage.

Upon retirement for service, a member shall receive a retirement allowance which shall consist of an annuity which shall be the actuarial equivalent of his accumulated deductions at the time of his retirement and a pension, in addition to his annuity, which shall be equal to one service-fraction of his final compensation, multiplied by the number of years of service since he last became a member credited to him, and a pension which is the actuarial equivalent of the reserve-for-increased-take-home-pay to which he may then be entitled, if any.

24. According to the above passage, a retirement allowance shall consist of a(n) 24.____
    A. annuity, plus a pension, plus an actuarial equivalent
    B. annuity, plus a pension, plus reserve-for-increased-take-home-pay, if any
    C. annuity, plus reserve-for-increased-take-home-pay, if any, plus final compensation
    D. pension, plus reserve-for-increased-take-home-pay, if any, plus accumulated deductions

Question 25.

DIRECTIONS: Question 25 is to be answered SOLELY on the basis of the following passage.

Membership in the retirement system shall cease upon the occurrence of any one of the following conditions: when the time out of service of any member who has total service of less than 25 years, shall aggregate more than 5 years; when the time out of service of any member who has total service of 25 years or more, shall aggregate more than 10 years; when any member shall have withdrawn more than 50% of his accumulated deductions; or when any member shall have withdrawn the cash benefit provided by Section B3.35.0 of the Administrative Code.

25. According to the information in the above passage, membership in the 25.____
    retirement system shall cease when an employee
    A. with 17 years of service has been on a leave of absence for 3 years
    B. withdraws 50% of his accumulated deductions
    C. with 28 years of service has been out of service for 10 years
    D. withdraws his cash benefits

KEY (CORRECT ANSWERS)

1.	B		11.	B
2.	A		12.	C
3.	C		13.	B
4.	A		14.	B
5.	D		15.	D
6.	B		16.	B
7.	A		17.	A
8.	C		18.	A
9.	B		19.	C
10.	C		20.	D

21.	B
22.	C
23.	D
24.	B
25.	D

TEST 2

DIRECTIONS: Each question or incomplete statement is followed by several suggested answers or completions. Select the one that BEST answers the question or completes the statement. *PRINT THE LETTER OF THE CORRECT ANSWER IN THE SPACE AT THE RIGHT.*

Questions 1-6.

DIRECTIONS: Questions 1 through 6 are to be answered SOLELY on the basis of the following passage.

    Since almost every office has some contact with data-processed records, a stenographer should have some understanding of the basic operations of data processing. Data processing systems now handle a vast majority of all office paperwork. On coded forms and other specialized media, data are recorded before being fed into the computer for processing. The data written on the source document is converted in highly advanced ways in order to make the information accessible to the user. After data has been converted, it must be verified to guarantee absolute accuracy. In this manner, data becomes a permanent record which can be read by computers that compare, store, compute, and otherwise process data at high speeds.

    One key person in a computer installation is a programmer, the man or woman who puts business and scientific problems into special symbolic languages that can be read by the computer. Jobs done by the computer range all the way from payroll operations to chemical process control, but most computer applications are directed toward management data. Most programmers employed by business come to their positions with college degrees; the rest are promoted to their positions from within the organization on the basis of demonstrated ability without regard to education.

1. Of the following, the BEST title for the above passage is 1.____
   A. The Stenographer As Data Processor
   B. The Relation of Data Input to Stenography
   C. Understanding Data Processing
   D. Permanent Office Records

2. According to the above passage, a stenographer should understand the basic 2.____
   operations of data processing because
   A. almost every office today has contact with data processed by computer
   B. any office worker may be asked to verify the accuracy of data
   C. most offices are involved in the production of permanent records
   D. data may be converted into computer language by specialized media

3. According to the above passage, data accuracy is reviewed during the _____ 3.____
   stage.
   A. processing
   B. verification
   C. programming
   D. stenographic

4. According to the above passage, computers are used MOST often to handle   4.____
   A. management data
   B. problems of higher education
   C. the control of chemical processes
   D. payroll operations

5. Computer programming is taught in many colleges and business schools.   5.____
   The above passage implies that programmers in industry
   A. must have professional training
   B. need professional training to advance
   C. must have at least a college education to do adequate programming tasks
   D. do not necessarily need college education to do programming work

6. According to the above passage, data to be processed by computer should be   6.____
   A. recent   B. basic   C. complete   D. verified

Questions 7-10.

DIRECTIONS: Questions 7 through 10 are to be answered SOLELY on the basis of the following passage.

There is nothing that will take the place of good sense on the part of the stenographer. You may be perfect in transcribing exactly what the dictator says and your speed may be adequate, but without an understanding of the dictator's intent as well as his words, you are likely to be a mediocre secretary.

A serious error that is made when taking dictation is putting down something that does not make sense. Most people who dictate material would rather be asked to repeat and explain than to receive transcribed material which has errors due to inattention or doubt. Many dictators request that their grammar be corrected by their secretaries, but unless specifically asked to do so, secretaries should not do it without first checking with the dictator. Secretaries should be aware that, in some cases, dictators may use incorrect grammar or slang expressions to create a particular effect.

Some people dictate commas, periods, and paragraphs, while others expect the stenographer to know when, where, and how to punctuate. A well-trained secretary should be able to indicate the proper punctuation by listening to the pauses and tones of the dictator's voice.

A stenographer who has taken dictation from the same person for a period of time should be able to understand him under most conditions. By increasing her tack, alertness, and efficiency, a secretary can become more competent.

7. According to the above passage, which of the following statements concerning   7.____
   the dictation of punctuation is CORRECT?
   A. Dictator may use incorrect punctuation to create a desired style.
   B. Dictator should indicate all punctuation.

C. Stenographer should know how to punctuate based on the pauses and tones of the dictator.
D. Stenographer should not type any punctuation if it has not been dictated to her.

8. According to the above passage, how should secretaries handle grammatical errors in a dictation?
Secretaries should
   A. *not correct* grammatical errors unless the dictator is aware that this is being done
   B. *correct* grammatical errors by having the dictator repeat the line with proper pauses
   C. *correct* grammatical errors if they have checked the correctness in a grammar book
   D. *correct* grammatical errors based on their own good sense

8.____

9. If a stenographer is confused about the method of spacing and indenting of a report which has just been dictated to her, she GENERALLY should
   A. do the best she can
   B. ask the dictator to explain what she should do
   C. try to improve her ability to understand dictated material
   D. accept the fact that her stenographic ability is not adequate

9.____

10. In the last line of the first paragraph, the word *mediocre* means MOST NEARLY
    A. superior   B. respected   C. disregarded   D. second-rate

10.____

Questions 11-12.

DIRECTIONS: Questions 11 and 12 are to be answered SOLELY on the basis of the following passage.

The number of legible carbon copies required to be produced determines the weight of the carbon paper to be used. When only one copy is made, heavy carbon paper is satisfactory. Most typists, however, use medium-weight carbon paper and find it serviceable for up to three or four copies. If five or more copies are to be made, it is wise to use light carbon paper. On the other hand, the finish of carbon paper to be used depends largely on the stroke of the typist and, in lesser degree, on the number of copies to be made and on whether the typewriter has pica or elite type. A soft-finish carbon paper should be used if the typist's touch is light or if a noiseless machine is used. It is desirable for the average typist to use medium-finish carbon paper for ordinary work, when only a few carbon copies are required. Elite type requires a harder carbon finish than pica type for the same number of copies.

11. According to the above passage, the lighter the carbon paper used, the
    A. softer the finish of the carbon paper will be
    B. greater the number of legible carbon copies that can be made
    C. greater the number of times the carbon paper can be used
    D. lighter the typist's touch should be

11.____

12. According to the above passage, the MOST important factor which determines whether the finish of carbon paper to be used in typing should be hard, medium, or soft is
    A. the touch of the typist
    B. the number of carbon copies required
    C. whether the type in the typewriter is pica or elite
    D. whether a machine with pica type will produce the same number of carbon copies as a machine with elite type

12._____

Questions 13-16.

DIRECTIONS: Questions 13 through 16 are to be answered SOLELY on the basis of the following passage.

Looking back at past developments in office work, advances were made at higher speeds and at greater efficiency thanks largely to the typewriter. The typewriter was a substitute for handwriting and, in the hands of a skilled typist, not only turned out letters and other documents at least three times faster than a penman, but turned out the greater volume more uniformly and legibly. With the use of carbon paper and onionskin paper, identical copies could be made at the same time.

The typewriter, besides its effect on the conduct of business and government, had a very important effect on the position of women. The typewriter did much to bring women into business and government, and in a short time span, women far outnumbered men as typists. Many women used the keys of the typewriter to climb the ladder to professional managerial positions.

The typewriter, as its name implies, employs type to make an ink impression on paper. For many years, the manual typewriter was the standard machine used. Eventually, the electric typewriter became dominant, leading to innovations in and widespread use of completely automatic electronic typewriters.

The mechanism of the office manual typewriter includes a set of keys arranged systematically in rows; a semicircular frame of type, connected to the keys by levers; the carriage, or paper carrier; a rubber roller, called a platen, against which the type strikes; and an inked ribbon which makes the impression of the type character when the key strikes it.

13. The above passage mentions a number of good features of the combination of a skilled typist and a typewriter.
    Of the following the feature which is NOT mentioned in the passage is
    A. speed   B. reliability   C. uniformity   D. legibility

13._____

14. According to the above passage, a skilled typist can
    A. turn out at least five carbon copies of typed matter
    B. type at least three times faster than a penman can write
    C. type more than 80 words in a minute
    D. readily move into a managerial position

14._____

15. According to the above passage, which of the following is NOT part of the mechanism of a manual typewriter?
    A. Carbon paper
    B. Platen
    C. Paper carrier
    D. Inked ribbon

15.____

16. According to the above passage, the typewriter helped
    A. men more than women in business
    B. women in career advancement into management
    C. men and women equally, but women have taken better advantage of it
    D. more women than men, because men generally dislike routine typing work

16.____

Questions 17-21.

DIRECTIONS: Questions 17 through 21 are to be answered SOLELY on the basis of the following passage.

The recipient gains an impression of a typewritten letter before he begins to read the message. Factors which provide for a good first impression include margins and spacing that are visually pleasing, formal parts of the letter which are correctly placed according to the style of the letter, copy which is free of obvious erasures and over-strikes, and transcript that is even and clear. The problem for the typist is that of how to produce that first, positive impression of her work.

There are several general rules which a typist can follow when she wishes to prepare a properly spaced letter on a sheet of letterhead. Ordinarily, the width of a letter should not be less than four inches nor more than six inches. The side margins should also have a desirable relation to the bottom margin and the space between the letterhead and the body of the letter. Usually the most appealing arrangement is when the side margins are even and the bottom margin is slightly wider than the side margins. In some offices, however, standard line length is used for all business letter, and the secretary then varies the spacing between the date line and the inside address according to the length of the letter.

17. The BEST title for the above passage would be
    A. Writing Office Letters
    B. Making Good First Impressions
    C. Judging Well-Typed Letters
    D. Good Placing and Spacing for Office Letters

17.____

18. According to the above passage, which of the following might be considered the way in which people very quickly judge the quality of work which has been typed? By
    A. measuring the margins to see if they are correct
    B. looking at the spacing and cleanliness of the typescript
    C. scanning the body of the letter for meaning
    D. reading the date line and address for errors

18.____

19. What, according to the above passage, would be definitely UNDESIRABLE as the average line length of a typed letter? 19.____
    A. 4"   B. 6"   C. 5"   D. 7"

20. According to the above passage, when the line length is kept standard, the secretary 20.____
    A. does not have to vary the spacing at all since this also is standard
    B. adjusts the spacing between the date line and inside address for different lengths of letters
    C. uses the longest line as a guidance for spacing between the date line and inside address
    D. varies the number of spaces between the lines

21. According to the above passage, side margins are MOST pleasing when they 21.____
    A. are even and somewhat smaller than the bottom margin
    B. are slightly wider than the bottom margin
    C. vary with the length of the letter
    D. are figured independently from the letterhead and the body of the letter

Questions 22-25.

DIRECTIONS: Questions 22 through 25 are to be answered SOLELY on the basis of the following passage.

Typed pages can reflect the simplicity of modern art in a machine age. Lightness and evenness can be achieved by proper layout and balance of typed lines and white space. Instead of solid, cramped masses of uneven, crowded typing, there should be a pleasing balance up and down as well as horizontal.

To have real balance, your page must have a center. The eyes see the center of the sheet slightly above the real center. This is the way both you and the reader see it. Try imagining a line down the center of the page that divides the paper in equal halves. On either side of your paper, white space and blocks of typing need to be similar in size and shape. Although left and right margins should be equal, top and bottom margins need not be as exact. It looks better to hold a bottom border wider than a top margin, so that your typing rests upon a cushion of white space. To add interest to the appearance of the page, try making one paragraph between one-half and two-thirds the size of an adjacent paragraph.

Thus, by taking full advantage of your typewriter, the pages that you type will not only be accurate but will also be attractive.

22. It can be inferred from the above passage that the basic importance of proper balancing on a typed page is that proper balancing 22.____
    A. makes a typed page a work of modern art
    B. provides exercise in proper positioning of a typewriter
    C. increases the amount of typed copy on the paper
    D. draws greater attention and interest to the page

23. A reader will tend to see the center of a typed page   23.____
    A. somewhat higher than the true center
    B. somewhat lower than the true center
    C. on either side of the true center
    D. about two-thirds of an inch above the true center

24. Which of the following suggestions is NOT given by the above passage?   24.____
    A. Bottom margins may be wider than top borders.
    B. Keep all paragraphs approximately the same size.
    C. Divide your page with an imaginary line down the middle.
    D. Side margins should be equalized.

25. Of the following, the BEST title for the above passage is   25.____
    A. Increasing the Accuracy of the Typed Page
    B. Determination of Margins for Typed Copy
    C. Layout and Balance of the Typed Page
    D. How to Take Full Advantage of the Typewriter

KEY (CORRECT ANSWERS)

1.	C	11.	B
2.	A	12.	A
3.	B	13.	B
4.	A	14.	B
5.	D	15.	A
6.	D	16.	B
7.	C	17.	D
8.	A	18.	B
9.	B	19.	D
10.	D	20.	B

21.	A
22.	D
23.	A
24.	B
25.	C

TEST 3

DIRECTIONS: Each question or incomplete statement is followed by several suggested answers or completions. Select the one that BEST answers the question or completes the statement. *PRINT THE LETTER OF THE CORRECT ANSWER IN THE SPACE AT THE RIGHT.*

Questions 1-5.

DIRECTIONS: Questions 1 through 5 are to be answered SOLELY on the basis of the following passage.

    A written report is a communication of information from one person to another. It is an account of some matter especially investigated, however routine that matter may be. The ultimate basis of any good written report is facts, which become known through observation and verification. Good written reports may seem to be no more than general ideas and opinions. However, in such cases, the facts leading too these opinions were gathered, verified, and reported earlier, and the opinions are dependent upon these facts. Good style, proper form, and emphasis cannot make a good written report out of unreliable information and bad judgment; but on the other hand, solid investigation and brilliant thinking are not likely to become very useful until they are effectively communicated to others. If a person's work calls for written reports, then his work is often no better than his written reports.

1. Based on the information in the above passage, it can be concluded that opinions expressed in a report should be
   A. based on facts which are gathered and reported
   B. emphasized repeatedly when they result from a special investigation
   C. kept to a minimum
   D. separated from the body of the report

   1.____

2. In the above passage, the one of the following which is mentioned as a way of establishing facts is
   A. authority
   B. reporting
   C. communication
   D. verification

   2.____

3. According to the above passage, the characteristic shared by ALL written reports is that they are
   A. accounts of routine matters
   B. transmissions of information
   C. reliable and logical
   D. written in proper form

   3.____

4. Which of the following conclusions can logically be drawn from the information given in the above passage?
   A. Brilliant thinking can make up for unreliable information in a report.
   B. One method of judging an individual's work is the quality of the written reports he is required to submit.
   C. Proper form and emphasis can make a good report out of unreliable information.
   D. Good written reports that seem to be no more than general ideas should be rewritten.

   4.____

5. Which of the following suggested titles would be MOST appropriate for the above passage? 5.____
   A. Gathering and Organizing Facts
   B. Techniques of Observation
   C. Nature and Purpose of Reports
   D. Reports and Opinions: Differences and Similarities

Questions 6-8.

DIRECTIONS: Questions 6 through 8 are to be answered SOLELY on the basis of the following passage.

The most important unit of the mimeograph machine is a perforated metal drum over which is stretched a cloth ink pad. A reservoir inside the drum contains the ink which flows through the perforations and saturates the ink pad. To operate the machine, the operator first removes from the machine the protective sheet, which keeps the ink from drying while the machine is not in use. He then hooks the stencil face down on the drum, draws the stencil smoothly over the drum, and fastens the stencil at the bottom. The speed with which the drum turns determines the blackness of the copies printed. Slow turning gives heavy, black copies; fast turning gives light, clear-cut reproductions. If reproductions are run on other than porous paper, slip-sheeting is necessary to prevent smearing. Often, the printed copy fails to drop readily as it comes from the machine. This may be due to static electricity. To remedy this difficulty, the operator fastens a strip of tinsel from side to side near the impression roller so that the printed copy just touches the soft stems of the tinsel as it is ejected from the machine, thus grounding the static electricity to the frame of the machine.

6. According to the above passage, 6.____
   A. turning the drum fast produces light copies
   B. stencils should be placed face up on the drum
   C. ink pads should be changed daily
   D. slip-sheeting is necessary when porous paper is being used

7. According to the above passage, when a mimeograph machine is not in use, the 7.____
   A. ink should be drained from the drum
   B. ink pad should be removed
   C. machine should be covered with a protective sheet
   D. counter should be set at zero

8. According to the above passage, static electricity is grounded to the frame of the mimeograph machine by means of 8.____
   A. a slip-sheeting device
   B. a strip of tinsel
   C. an impression roller
   D. hooks located at the top of the drum

Questions 9-10.

DIRECTIONS: Questions 9 and 10 are to be answered SOLELY on the basis of the following passage.

The proofreading of material typed from copy is performed more accurately and more speedily when two persons perform this work as a team. The person who did not do the typing should read aloud the original copy while the person who did the typing should check the reading against the typed copy. The reader should speak very slowly and repeat the figures, using a different grouping of number when repeating the figures. For example, in reading 1967, the reader may say *one-nine-six-seven* on first reading the figure and *nineteen-sixty-seven* on repeating the figure. The reader should read all punctuation marks, taking nothing for granted. Since mistakes can occur anywhere, everything typed should be proofread. To avoid confusion, the proofreading team should use the standard proofreading marks, which are given in most dictionaries.

9. According to the above passage, the
  A. person who holds the typed copy is called the reader
  B. two members of a proofreading team should take turns in reading the typed copy aloud
  C. typed copy should be checked by the person who did the typing
  D. person who did not do the typing should read aloud from the typed copy

9.____

10. According to the above passage,
  A. it is unnecessary to read the period at the end of a sentence
  B. typographical errors should be noted on the original copy
  C. each person should develop his own set of proofreading marks
  D. figures should be read twice

10.____

Questions 11-16.

DIRECTIONS: Questions 11 through 16 are to be answered SOLELY on the basis of the following passage.

Basic to every office is the need for proper lighting. Inadequate lighting is a familiar cause of fatigue and serves to create a somewhat dismal atmosphere in the office. One requirement of proper lighting is that it be of an appropriate intensity. Intensity is measured in foot-candles. According to the Illuminating Engineering Society of New York, for casual seeing tasks such as in reception rooms, inactive file rooms, and other service areas, it is recommending that the amount of light be 30 foot-candle. For ordinary seeing tasks such as reading, work in active file rooms, and in mailrooms, the recommended lighting is 100 foot-candles. For very difficult seeing tasks such as accounting, transcribing, and business machine use, the recommended lighting is 150 foot-candles.

Lighting intensity is only one requirement. Shadows and glare are to be avoided. For example, the larger the proportion of a ceiling filled with lighting units, the more glare-free and comfortable the lighting will be. Natural lighting from window is not too dependable because on dark wintry days, windows yield little usable light, and on sunny afternoons, the glare from windows may be very distracting. Desks should not face the windows. Finally, the main lighting source ought to be overhead and to the left of the user.

11. According to the above passage, insufficient light in the office may cause 11.____
    A. glare   B. tiredness   C. shadows   D. distraction

12. Based on the above passage, which of the following must be considered when planning lighting arrangements? The 12.____
    A. amount of natural light present
    B. amount of work to be done
    C. level of difficulty of work to be done
    D. type of activity to be carried out

13. It can be inferred from the above passage that a well-coordinated lighting scheme is LIKELY to result in 13.____
    A. greater employee productivity   B. elimination of light reflection
    C. lower lighting cost   D. more use of natural light

14. Of the following, the BEST title for the above passage is 14.____
    A. Characteristics of Light
    B. Light Measurement Devices
    C. Factors to Consider When Planning Lighting Systems
    D. comfort vs. Cost When Devising Lighting Arrangements

15. According to the above passage, a foot-candle is a measurement of the 15.____
    A. number of bulbs used
    B. strength of the light
    C. contrast between glare and shadow
    D. proportion of the ceiling filled with lighting units

16. According to the above passage, the number of foot-candles of light that would be needed to copy figures onto a payroll is _____ foot-candles. 16.____
    A. less than 30   B. 100   C. 30   D. 140

Questions 17-23.

DIRECTIONS: Questions 17 through 23 are to be answered SOLELY on the basis of the following passage.

FEE SCHEDULE

1. A candidate for any baccalaureate degree is not required to pay tuition fees for undergraduate courses until he exceeds 128 credits. Candidates exceeding 128 credits in undergraduate courses are charged at the rate of $100 a credit for each credit of undergraduate course work in excess of 128. Candidates for a baccalaureate degree who are taking graduate courses must pay the same fee as any other student taking graduate courses.

5 (#3)

B. Non-degree students and college graduates are charged tuition fees for courses, whether undergraduate or graduate, at the rate of $180 a credit. For such students, there is an additional charge of $150 for each class hour per week in excess of the number of course credits. For example, if a three-credit course meets five hours a week, there is an additional charge for the extra two hours. Graduate courses are shown with a (G) before the course number.

C. All students are required to pay the laboratory fees indicated after the number of credits given for that course.

D. All students must pay a $250 general fee each semester.

E. Candidates for a baccalaureate degree are charged a $150 medical insurance fee for each semester. All other students are charged a $100 medical insurance fee each semester.

17. Miss Burton is not a candidate for a degree. She registers for the following courses in the spring semester: Economics 12, 4 hours a week, 3 credits; History (G 23, 4 hours a week, 3 credits; English 1, 2 hours a week, 2 credits. The TOTAL amount in fees that Miss Burton must pay is
    A. less than $2,000
    B. at least $2,000 but less than $2,100
    C. at least $2,100 but less than $2,200
    D. $2,200 or over

17.____

18. Miss Gray is not a candidate for a degree. She registers for the following courses in the fall semester: History 3, 3 hours a week, 3 credits; English 5, 3 hours a week, 2 credits; Physics 5, 6 hours a week, 3 credits, laboratory fee $60; Mathematics 7, 4 hours a week, 3 credits.
    The TOTAL amount in fees that Miss Gray must pay is
    A. less than $3,150
    B. at least $3,150 but less than $3,250
    C. at least $3,250 but less than $3,350
    D. $3,350 or over

18.____

19. Mr. Wall is a candidate for the Bachelor of Arts degree and has completed 126 credits. He registers for the following courses in the spring semester, his final semester at college; French 4, 3 hours a week, 3 credits; Physics (G) 15, 6 hours a week, 3 credits, laboratory fee $80; History (G) 33, 4 hours a week, 3 credits.
    The TOTAL amount in fees that this candidate must pay is
    A. less than $2,100
    B. at least $2,100 but less than $2,300
    C. at least $2,300 but less than $2,500
    D. $2,500

19.____

6 (#3)

20. Mr. Tindall, a candidate for the B.A. degree, has completed 122 credits of undergraduate courses. He registers for the following courses in his final semester: English 31, 3 hours a week, 3 credits; Philosophy 12, 4 hours a week, 4 credits; Anthropology 15, 3 hours a week, 3 credits; Economics (G) 68, 3 hours a week, 3 credits.
    The TOTAL amount in fees that Mr. Tindall must pay in his final semester is
    A. less than $1,200
    B. at least $1,200 but less than $1,400
    C. at least $1,400 but less than $1,600
    D. $1,600

20.____

21. Mr. Cantrell, who was graduated from the college a year ago, registers for graduate courses in the fall semester. Each course for which he register carries the same number of credits as the number of hours a week it meets. If he pays a total of $1,530, including a $100 laboratory fee, the number of credits for which he is registered is
    A. 4   B. 5   C. 6   D. 7

21.____

22. Miss Jayson, who is not a candidate for a degree, has registered for several courses including a lecture course in History. She withdraws from the course in History for which she had paid the required course fee of $690.
    The number of hours that this course is scheduled to meet is
    A. 4   B. 5   C. 2   D. 3

22.____

23. Mr. Van Arsdale, a graduate of a college in Iowa, registers for the following courses in one semester: Chemistry 35, 5 hours a week, 3 credits; Biology 14, 4 hours a week, 3 credits, laboratory fee $150; Mathematics (G) 179, 3 hours a week, 3 credits.
    The TOTAL amount in fees that Mr. Van Arsdale must pay is
    A. less than $2,400
    B. at least $2,400 but less than $2,500
    C. at least $2,500 but less than $2,600
    D. at least $2,600 or over

23.____

Questions 24-25.

DIRECTIONS: Questions 24 and 25 are to be answered SOLELY on the basis of the following passage.

A duplex envelope is an envelope composed of two sections securely fastened together so that they become one mailing piece. This type of envelope makes it possible for a first class letter to be delivered simultaneously with third or fourth class matter and yet not require payment of the much higher first class postage rate on the entire mailing. First class postage is paid only on the letter which goes in the small compartment, third or fourth class postage being paid on the contents of the larger compartment. The larger compartment generally has an ungummed flap or clasp for sealing. The first class or smaller compartment has a gummed flap for sealing. Postal regulations require that the exact amount of postage applicable to each compartment be separately attached to it.

24. On the basis of the above passage, it is MOST accurate to state that   24.____
    A. the smaller compartment is placed inside the larger compartment before mailing
    B. the two compartments may be detached and mailed separately
    C. two classes of mailing matter may be mailed as a unit at two different postage rates
    D. the more expensive postage rate is paid on the matter in the larger compartment

25. When a duplex envelope is used, the   25.____
    A. first class compartment may be sealed with a clasp
    B. correct amount of postage must be placed on each compartment
    C. compartment containing third or fourth class mail requires a gummed flap for sealing
    D. full amount of postage for both compartments may be placed on the larger compartment

---

KEY (CORRECT ANSWERS)

1.	A		11.	C
2.	D		12.	D
3.	B		13.	A
4.	B		14.	C
5.	C		15.	B
6.	A		16.	D
7.	C		17.	B
8.	B		18.	A
9.	C		19.	B
10.	D		20.	B

21. C
22. A
23. C
24. C
25. B

DOCUMENTS AND FORMS
PREPARING WRITTEN MATERIALS
EXAMINATION SECTION
TEST 1

DIRECTIONS: Each question or incomplete statement is followed by several suggested answers or completions. Select the one that BEST answers the question or completes the statement. *PRINT THE LETTER OF THE CORRECT ANSWER IN THE SPACE AT THE RIGHT.*

1. Of the following types of documents, it is MOST important to retain and file
    A. working drafts of reports that have been submitted in final form
    B. copies of letters of good will which conveyed a message that could not be handled by phone
    C. interoffice orders for materials which have been received and verified
    D. interoffice memoranda regarding the routine of standard forms

2. The MAXIMUM number of 2¾" x 4¼" size forms which may be obtained from one ream of 17" x 22" paper is
    A. 4,000   B. 8,000   C. 12,000   D. 16,000

3. On a general organization chart, staff positions NORMALLY should be pictured
    A. directly above the line positions to which they report
    B. to the sides of the main flow lines
    C. within the box of the highest level subordinate positions pictured
    D. directly below the line positions which report to them

4. When an administrator is diagramming an office layout, of the following, his PRIMARY job generally should be to indicate the
    A. lighting intensities that will be required by each operator
    B. noise level that will be produced by the various equipment employed in the office
    C. direction of the work flow and the distance involved in each transfer
    D. durability of major pieces of office equipment currently in use or to be utilized

5. One common guideline or rule-of-thumb ratio for evaluating the efficiency of files is the number of records requested divided by the number of records filed. Generally, if this ratio is very low, it would point MOST directly to the need for
    A. improving the indexing and coding systems
    B. improving the charge-out procedures
    C. exploring the need for transferring records from active storage to the archives
    D. exploring the need to encourage employees to keep more records in their private files

6. The GREATEST percentage of money spent on preparing and keeping the usual records in an office generally is expended for which one of the following?
   A. Renting space in which to place the record-keeping equipment
   B. Paying salaries of record-preparing and record-keeping personnel
   C. Depreciation of purchased record-preparation and record-keeping machines
   D. Paper and forms upon which to place the records

7. In a certain office, file folders are constantly being removed from the files for use by administrators. At the same time, new material is coming in to be filed in some of these folders.
   Of the following, the BEST way to avoid delays in filing of the new material and to keep track of the removed folders is to
   A. keep a sheet listing all folders removed from the file, who has them, and a follow-update to check on their return; attach to this list new material received for filing
   B. put an "out" slip in the place of any file folder removed, telling what folder is missing, date removed, and who has it; file new material received at front of files
   C. put a temporary "out" folder in place of the one removed, giving title or subject, date removed, and who has it; put into this temporary folder any new material received
   D. keep a list of all folders removed and who has them; forward any new material received for filing while a folder is out to the person who has it

8. Folders labeled "Miscellaneous" should be used in an alphabetic filing system MAINLY to
   A. provide quick access to recent material
   B. avoid setting up individual folders for infrequent correspondence
   C. provide temporary storage for less important documents
   D. temporarily hold papers which will not fit into already crowded individual folders

9. Out-of-date and seldom-used records should be removed periodically from the files because
   A. overall responsibility for records will be transferred to the person in charge of the central storage files
   B. duplicate copies of every record are not needed
   C. valuable filing space will be regained and the time needed to find a current record will be cut down
   D. worthwhile suggestions on improving the filing system will result whenever this is done

10. Of the following, the BEST reason for discarding certain material from office files would be that the
    A. files are crowded
    B. material in the files is old
    C. material duplicates information obtainable from other sources in the files
    D. material is referred to most often by employees in an adjoining office

3 (#1)

11. Of the following, the MAIN factor contributing to the expense of maintaining an office procedure manual would be the
   A. infrequent use of the manual
   B. need to revise it regularly
   C. cost of loose-leaf binders
   D. high cost of printing

11.____

12. The suggestion that memos or directives which circulate among subordinates be initialed by each employee is a
   A. *poor* one, because, with modern copying machines, it would be possible to supply every subordinate with a copy of each message for his personal use
   B. *good* one, because it relieves the supervisor of blame for the action of subordinates who have read and initialed the messages
   C. *poor* one, because initialing the memo or directive is no guarantee that the subordinate has read the material
   D. *good* one, because it can be used as a record by the supervisor to show that his subordinates have received the message and were responsible for reading it

12.____

13. Of the following, the MOST important reason for microfilming office records is to
   A. save storage space needed to keep records
   B. make it easier to get records when needed
   C. speed up the classification of information
   D. shorten the time which records must be kept

13.____

14. Your office filing cabinets have become so overcrowded that it is difficult to use the files.
   Of the following, the MOST desirable step for you to take FIRST to relieve this situation would be to
   A. assign your assistant to spend some time each day reviewing the material in the files and to give you his recommendations as to what material may be discarded
   B. discard all material which has been in the files more than a given number of years
   C. submit a request for additional filing cabinets in your next budget request
   D. transfer enough material to the central storage room of your agency to give you the amount of additional filing space needed

14.____

15. In indexing names of business firms and other organizations, one of the rules to be followed is:
   A. The word "and" is considered an indexing unit
   B. When a firm name includes the full name of a person who is not well known, the person's first name is considered as the first indexing unit
   C. Usually, the units in a firm name are indexed in the order in which they are written
   D. When a firm's name is made up of single letters (such as ABC Corp.), the letters taken together are considered as more than one indexing unit

15.____

16. Assume that your unit processes confidential forms which are submitted by persons seeking financial assistance. An individual comes to your office, gives you his name, and states that he would like to look over a form which he sent in about a week ago because he believes he omitted some important information.
    Of the following, the BEST thing for you to do FIRST is to
    A. locate the proper form
    B. call the individual's home telephone number to verify his identity
    C. ask the individual if he has proof of his identity
    D. call the security office

17. An employee has been assigned to open her division head's mail and place it on his desk. One day, the employee opens a letter which she then notices is marked "Personal."
    Of the following, the BEST action for her to take is to
    A. write "Personal" on the letter and staple the envelope to the back of the letter
    B. ignore the matter and treat the letter the same way as the others
    C. give it to another division head to hold until her own division head comes into the office
    D. leave the letter in the envelope and write "Sorry-opened by mistake" on the envelope, and initial it

18. The MOST important reason for having a filing system is to
    A. get papers out of the way
    B. have a record of everything that has happened
    C. retain information to justify your actions
    D. enable rapid retrieval of information

19. The system of filing which is used MOST frequently is called _____ filing.
    A. alphabetic   B. alphanumeric
    C. geographic   D. numeric

20. In judging the adequacy of a standard office form, which of the following is LEAST important?
    A. Date of the form   B. Legibility of the form
    C. Size of the form   D. Design of the form

21. Assume that the letters and reports which are dictated to you fall into a few distinct subject-matter areas.
    The practice of trying to familiarize yourself with the terminology in these areas is
    A. *good*, because you will have a basis for commenting on the dictated material
    B. *good*, because it will be easier to take the dictation at the rate at which it is given
    C. *poor*, because the functions and policies of an office are not of your concern
    D. *poor*, because it will take too much time away from your assigned work

22. A letter was dictated on June 9 and was ready to be typed on June 12. The letter was typed on June 13, signed on June 14, and mailed on June 14. The date that, ORDINARILY, should have appeared on the letter is June
    A. 9   B. 12   C. 13   D. 14

23. Of the following, the BEST reason for putting the "key point" at the beginning of a letter is that it
    A. may save time for the reader
    B. is standard practice in writing letters
    C. will more likely to be typed correctly
    D. cannot logically be placed elsewhere

24. As a supervisor, you have been asked to attend committee meetings and take the minutes.
    The body of such minutes GENERALLY consists of
    A. the date and place of the meeting and the list of persons present
    B. an exact verbatim report of everything that was said by each person who spoke
    C. a clear description of each matter discussed and the action decided on
    D. the agenda of the meeting

25. When typing a rough draft from a recorded transcription, a stenographer under your supervision reaches a spot on the recording that is virtually inaudible.
    Of the following, the MOST advisable action that you should recommend to her is to
    A. guess what the dictator intended to say based on what he said in the parts that are clear
    B. ask the dictator to listen to his unsatisfactory recording
    C. leave an appropriate amount of space for that portion that is inaudible
    D. stop typing the draft and send a note to the dictator identifying the item that could not be completed

KEY (CORRECT ANSWERS)

1. D
2. D
3. B
4. C
5. C

6. B
7. C
8. B
9. C
10. C

11. B
12. D
13. A
14. A
15. C

16. C
17. D
18. D
19. A
20. A

21. B
22. D
23. A
24. C
25. C

TEST 2

DIRECTIONS: Each question or incomplete statement is followed by several suggested answers or completions. Select the one that BEST answers the question or completes the statement. *PRINT THE LETTER OF THE CORRECT ANSWER IN THE SPACE AT THE RIGHT.*

1. To tell a newly employed clerk to fill a top drawer of a four-drawer cabinet with heavy binders which will be often used and to keep lower drawers only partly filled is
    A. *good*, because a tall person would have to bend unnecessarily if he had to use a lower drawer
    B. *bad*, because the file cabinet may tip over when the top drawer is opened
    C. *good*, because it is the most easily reachable drawer for the average person
    D. *bad*, because a person bending down at another drawer may accidentally bang his head on the bottom of the drawer when he straightens up

2. If you have requisitioned a "ream" of paper in order to duplicate a single page office announcement, how many announcements can be printed from the one package of paper?
    A. 200   B. 500   C. 700   D. 1,000

3. In the operations of a government agency, a voucher is ORDINARILY used to
    A. refer someone to the agency for a position or assignment
    B. certify that an agency's records of financial transactions are accurate
    C. order payment from agency funds of a stated amount to an individual
    D. enter a statement of official opinion in the records of the agency

4. Of the following types of cards used in filing systems, the one which is generally MOST helpful in locating records which might be filed under more than one subject is the _____ card.
    A. out
    B. tickler
    C. cross-reference
    D. visible index

5. The type of filing system in which one does NOT need to refer to a card index in order to find the folder is called
    A. alphabetic   B. geographic   C. subject   D. locational

6. Of the following, records management is LEAST concerned with
    A. the development of the best method for retrieving important information
    B. deciding what records should be kept
    C. deciding the number of appointments a client will need
    D. determining the types of folders to be used

7. If records are continually removed from a set of files without "charging" them to the borrower, the filing system will soon become ineffective.
Of the following terms, the one which is NOT applied to a form used in the charge-out system is a
   A. requisition card
   B. out-folder
   C. record retrieval form
   D. substitution card

8. A new clerk has been told to put 500 cards in alphabetical order. Another clerk suggests that she divide the cards into four groups, such as A to F, G to L, M to R, and S to Z, and then alphabetize these four smaller groups.
The suggested method is
   A. *poor*, because the clerk will have to handle the sheets more than once and will waste time
   B. *good*, because it saves time, is more accurate, and is less tiring
   C. *good*, because she will not have to concentrate on it so much when it is in smaller groups
   D. *poor*, because this method is much more tiring than straight alphabetizing

9. In Microsoft Excel, data and records are entered into
   A. pages   B. forms   C. cells   D. contracts

10. Suppose a clerk has been given pads of pre-printed forms to use when taking phone messages for others in her office. The clerk is then observed using scraps of paper and not the forms for writing her messages.
It should be explained that the BEST reason for using the forms is that
   A. they act as a checklist to make sure that the important information is taken
   B. she is expected to do her work in the same way as others in the office
   C. they make sure that unassigned paper is not wasted on phone messages
   D. learning to use these forms will help train her to use more difficult forms

11. The high-speed printing process used for producing large quantities of superior quality copy and cost efficiency is called
   A. photocopying
   B. laser printing
   C. inkjet printing
   D. word processing

12. Of the following, the MAIN reason a stock clerk keeps a perpetual inventory of supplies in the storeroom is that such an inventory will
   A. eliminate the need for a physical inventory
   B. provide a continuous record of supplies on hand
   C. indicate whether a shipment of supplies is satisfactory
   D. dictate the terms of the purchase order

13. As a supervisor, you may be required to handle different types of correspondence.
    Of the following types of letters, it would be MOST important to promptly seal which kind of letter?
    A. One marked "confidential"
    B. Those containing enclosures
    C. Any letter to be sent airmail
    D. Those in which copies will be sent along with the original

14. While opening incoming mail, you notice that one letter indicates that an enclosure was to be included but, even after careful inspection, you are not able to find the information to which this refers.
    Of the following, the thing that you should do FIRST is
    A. replace the letter in its envelope and return it to the sender
    B. file the letter until the sender's office mails the missing information
    C. type out a letter to the sender informing him of his error
    D. make a notation in the margin of the letter that the enclosure was omitted

15. You have been given a checklist and assigned the responsibility of inspecting certain equipment in the various offices of your agency.
    Which of the following is the GREATEST advantage of the checklist?
    A. It indicates which equipment is in greatest demand.
    B. Each piece of equipment on the checklist will be checked only once.
    C. It helps to insure that the equipment listed will not be overlooked.
    D. The equipment listed suggests other equipment you should look for.

16. The BEST way to evaluate the overall state of completion of a construction project is to check the progress estimate against the
    A. inspection worksheet   B. construction schedule
    C. inspector's checklist   D. equipment maintenance schedule

17. The usual contract for agency work includes a section entitled "Instructions to Bidders," which states that the
    A. contractor agrees that he has made his own examination and will make no claim for damages on account of errors or omissions
    B. contractor shall not make claims for damages of any discrepancy, error, or omission in any plans
    C. estimates of quantities and calculations are guaranteed by the agency to be correct and are deemed to be a representation of the conditions affecting the work
    D. plans, measurements, dimensions, and conditions under which the work is to be performed are guaranteed by the agency

18. In order to avoid disputes over payments for extra work in a contract for construction, the BEST procedure to follow would be to
    A. have contractor submit work progress reports daily
    B. insert a special clause in the contract specifications
    C. have a representative on the job at all times to verify conditions
    D. allocate a certain percentage of the cost of the job to cover such expenses

19. Prior to the installation of equipment called for in the specifications, the contractor is USUALLY required to submit for approval
    A. sets of shop drawings
    B. a set of revised specifications
    C. a detailed description of the methods of work to be used
    D. a complete list of skilled and unskilled tradesmen he proposes to use

20. During the actual construction work, the CHIEF value of a construction schedule is to
    A. insure that the work will be done on time
    B. reveal whether production is falling behind
    C. show how much equipment and material is required for the project
    D. furnish data as to the methods and techniques of construction operations

KEY (CORRECT ANSWERS)

1.	B	11.	B
2.	B	12.	B
3.	C	13.	A
4.	C	14.	D
5.	A	15.	C
6.	C	16.	B
7.	C	17.	A
8.	B	18.	C
9.	C	19.	A
10.	A	20.	B

PREPARING WRITTEN MATERIAL
EXAMINATION SECTION
TEST 1

DIRECTIONS: Each of the sentences in this test may be classified under one of the following four categories:
- A. Faulty because of incorrect grammar or word usage
- B. Faulty because of incorrect punctuation
- C. Faulty because of incorrect capitalization or incorrect spelling
- D. Correct

Examine each sentence carefully to determine under which of the above four options it is best classified. Then, in the space to the right, print the capital letter preceding the option which is the BEST of the four suggested above. (Note that each faulty sentence contains but one type of error. Consider a sentence to be correct if it contains none of the types of errors mentioned, even though there may be other correct ways of expressing the same thought.)

1. He sent the notice to the clerk who you hired yesterday.   1._____

2. It must be admitted, however that you were not informed of this change.   2._____

3. Only the employee who have served in this grade for at least two years are eligible for promotion.   3._____

4. The work was divided equally between she and Mary.   4._____

5. He thought that you were not available at that time.   5._____

6. When the messenger returns; please give him this package.   6._____

7. The new secretary prepared, typed, addressed, and delivered, the notices.   7._____

8. Walking into the room, his desk can be seen at the rear.   8._____

9. Although John has worked here longer than She, he produces a smaller amount of work.   9._____

10. She said she could of typed this report yesterday.   10._____

11. Neither one of these procedures are adequate for the efficient performance of this task.   11._____

12. The typewriter is the tool of the typist; the cash register, the tool of the cashier.   12._____

13. "The assignment must be completed as soon as possible" said the supervisor. 13.____

14. As you know, office handbooks are issued to all new Employees. 14.____

15. Writing a speech is sometimes easier than to deliver it before an audience. 15.____

16. Mr. Brown our accountant, will audit the accounts next week. 16.____

17. Give the assignment to whomever is able to do it most efficiently. 17.____

18. The supervisor expected either your or I to file these reports. 18.____

KEY (CORRECT ANSWERS)

1.	A	11.	A
2.	B	12.	C
3.	D	13.	B
4.	A	14.	C
5.	D	15.	A
6.	B	16.	B
7.	B	17.	A
8.	A	18.	A
9.	C		
10.	A		

TEST 2

DIRECTIONS: Each of the sentences in this test may be classified under one of the following four categories:
- A. Faulty because of incorrect grammar or word usage
- B. Faulty because of incorrect punctuation
- C. Faulty because of incorrect capitalization or incorrect spelling
- D. Correct

Examine each sentence carefully to determine under which of the above four options it is best classified. Then, in the space to the right, print the capital letter preceding the option which is the BEST of the four suggested above. (Note that each faulty sentence contains but one type of error. Consider a sentence to be correct if it contains none of the types of errors mentioned, even though there may be other correct ways of expressing the same thought.)

1. The fire apparently started in the storeroom, which is usually locked.   1.____
2. On approaching the victim, two bruises were noticed by this officer.   2.____
3. The officer, who was there examined the report with great care.   3.____
4. Each employee in the office had a seperate desk.   4.____
5. All employees including members of the clerical staff, were invited to the lecture.   5.____
6. The suggested Procedure is similar to the one now in use.   6.____
7. No one was more pleased with the new procedure than the chauffeur.   7.____
8. He tried to persaude her to change the procedure.   8.____
9. The total of the expenses charged to petty cash were high.   9.____
10. An understanding between him and I was finally reached.   10.____

KEY (CORRECT ANSWERS)

1.	D	6.	C
2.	A	7.	D
3.	B	8.	C
4.	C	9.	A
5.	B	10.	A

TEST 3

DIRECTIONS: Each of the sentences in this test may be classified under one of the following four categories:
- A. Faulty because of incorrect grammar or word usage
- B. Faulty because of incorrect punctuation
- C. Faulty because of incorrect capitalization or incorrect spelling
- D. Correct

Examine each sentence carefully to determine under which of the above four options it is best classified. Then, in the space to the right, print the capital letter preceding the option which is the BEST of the four suggested above. (Note that each faulty sentence contains but one type of error. Consider a sentence to be correct if it contains none of the types of errors mentioned, even though there may be other correct ways of expressing the same thought.)

1. They told both he and I that the prisoner had escaped. 1._____

2. Any superior officer, who, disregards the just complaint of his subordinates, is remiss in the performance of his duty. 2._____

3. Only those members of the national organization who resided in the Middle West attended the conference in Chicago. 3._____

4. We told him to give the national organization assignment to whoever was available. 4._____

5. Please do not disappoint and embarass us by not appearing in court. 5._____

6. Although the office's speech proved to be entertaining, the topic was not relevent to the main theme of the conference. 6._____

7. In February all new officers attended a training course in which they were learned in their principal duties and the fundamental operating procedure of the department. 7._____

8. I personally seen inmate Jones threaten inmates Smith and Green with bodily harm if they refused to participate in the plot. 8._____

9. To the layman, who on a chance visit to the prison observes everything functioning smoothly, the maintenance of prison discipline may seem to be a relatively easily realizable objective. 9._____

10. The prisoners in cell block fourty were forbidden to sit on the cell cots during the recreation hour. 10._____

KEY (CORRECT ANSWERS)

1. A
2. B
3. C
4. D
5. C
6. C
7. A
8. A
9. D
10. C

TEST 4

DIRECTIONS: Each of the sentences in this test may be classified under one of the following four categories:
   A. Faulty because of incorrect grammar or word usage
   B. Faulty because of incorrect punctuation
   C. Faulty because of incorrect capitalization or incorrect spelling
   D. Correct

Examine each sentence carefully to determine under which of the above four options it is best classified. Then, in the space to the right, print the capital letter preceding the option which is the BEST of the four suggested above. (Note that each faulty sentence contains but one type of error. Consider a sentence to be correct if it contains none of the types of errors mentioned, even though there may be other correct ways of expressing the same thought.)

1. I cannot encourage you any.   1._____
2. You always look well in those sort of clothes.   2._____
3. Shall we go to the park?   3._____
4. The man whome he introduced was Mr. Carey.   4._____
5. She saw the letter laying here this morning.   5._____
6. It should rain before the Afternoon is over.   6._____
7. They have already went home.   7._____
8. That Jackson will be elected is evident.   8._____
9. He does not hardly approve of us.   9._____
10. It was he, who won the prize.   10._____

KEY (CORRECT ANSWERS)

1. A   6. C
2. A   7. A
3. D   8. D
4. C   9. A
5. A   10. B

TEST 5

DIRECTIONS: Each of the sentences in this test may be classified under one of the following four categories:
  A. Faulty because of incorrect grammar or word usage
  B. Faulty because of incorrect punctuation
  C. Faulty because of incorrect capitalization or incorrect spelling
  D. Correct

Examine each sentence carefully to determine under which of the above four options it is best classified. Then, in the space to the right, print the capital letter preceding the option which is the BEST of the four suggested above. (Note that each faulty sentence contains but one type of error. Consider a sentence to be correct if it contains none of the types of errors mentioned, even though there may be other correct ways of expressing the same thought.)

1. Shall we go to the park. 1._____
2. They are, alike, in this particular way. 2._____
3. They gave the poor man sume food when he knocked on the door. 3._____
4. I regret the loss caused by the error. 4._____
5. The students' will have a new teacher. 5._____
6. They sweared to bring out all the facts. 6._____
7. He decided to open a branch store on 33rd street. 7._____
8. His speed is equal and more than that of a racehorse. 8._____
9. He felt very warm on that Summer day. 9._____
10. He was assisted by his friend, who lives in the next house. 10._____

KEY (CORRECT ANSWERS)

1.	B	6.	A
2.	B	7.	C
3.	C	8.	A
4.	D	9.	C
5.	B	10.	D

TEST 6

DIRECTIONS: Each of the sentences in this test may be classified under one of the following four categories:
- A. Faulty because of incorrect grammar or word usage
- B. Faulty because of incorrect punctuation
- C. Faulty because of incorrect capitalization or incorrect spelling
- D. Correct

Examine each sentence carefully to determine under which of the above four options it is best classified. Then, in the space to the right, print the capital letter preceding the option which is the BEST of the four suggested above. (Note that each faulty sentence contains but one type of error. Consider a sentence to be correct if it contains none of the types of errors mentioned, even though there may be other correct ways of expressing the same thought.)

1. The climate of New York is colder than California. 1._____
2. I shall wait for you on the corner. 2._____
3. Did we see the boy who, we think, is the leader. 3._____
4. Being a modest person, John seldom talks about his invention. 4._____
5. The gang is called the smith street bos. 5._____
6. He seen the man break into the store. 6._____
7. We expected to lay still there for quite a while. 7._____
8. He is considered to be the Leader of his organization. 8._____
9. Although I recieved an invitation, I won't go. 9._____
10. The letter must be here some place. 10._____

KEY (CORRECT ANSWERS)

1.	A	6.	A
2.	D	7.	A
3.	B	8.	C
4.	D	9.	C
5.	C	10.	A

TEST 7

DIRECTIONS: Each of the sentences in this test may be classified under one of the following four categories:
- A. Faulty because of incorrect grammar or word usage
- B. Faulty because of incorrect punctuation
- C. Faulty because of incorrect capitalization or incorrect spelling
- D. Correct

Examine each sentence carefully to determine under which of the above four options it is best classified. Then, in the space to the right, print the capital letter preceding the option which is the BEST of the four suggested above. (Note that each faulty sentence contains but one type of error. Consider a sentence to be correct if it contains none of the types of errors mentioned, even though there may be other correct ways of expressing the same thought.)

1. I though it to be he.   1.____
2. We expect to remain here for a long time.   2.____
3. The committee was agreed.   3.____
4. Two-thirds of the building are finished.   4.____
5. The water was froze.   5.____
6. Everyone of the salesmen must supply their own car.   6.____
7. Who is the author of Gone With the Wind?   7.____
8. He marched on and declaring that he would never surrender.   8.____
9. Who shall I say called?   9.____
10. Everyone has left but they.   10.____

KEY (CORRECT ANSWERS)

1.	A	6.	A
2.	D	7.	B
3.	D	8.	A
4.	A	9.	D
5.	A	10.	D

TEST 8

DIRECTIONS: Each of the sentences in this test may be classified under one of the following four categories:
  A. Faulty because of incorrect grammar or word usage
  B. Faulty because of incorrect punctuation
  C. Faulty because of incorrect capitalization or incorrect spelling
  D. Correct

Examine each sentence carefully to determine under which of the above four options it is best classified. Then, in the space to the right, print the capital letter preceding the option which is the BEST of the four suggested above. (Note that each faulty sentence contains but one type of error. Consider a sentence to be correct if it contains none of the types of errors mentioned, even though there may be other correct ways of expressing the same thought.)

1. Who did we give the order to?   1.____
2. Send your order in immediately.   2.____
3. I believe I paid the Bill.   3.____
4. I have not met but one person.   4.____
5. Why aren't Tom, and Fred, going to the dance?   5.____
6. What reason is there for him not going?   6.____
7. The seige of Malta was a tremendous event.   7.____
8. I was there yesterday I assure you   8.____
9. Your ukulele is better than mine.   9.____
10. No one was there only Mary.   10.____

KEY (CORRECT ANSWERS)

1.	A	6.	A
2.	D	7.	C
3.	C	8.	B
4.	A	9.	C
5.	B	10.	A

TEST 9

DIRECTIONS: In each of the following groups of sentences, one of the four sentences is faulty in grammar, punctuation, or capitalization. Select the INCORRECT sentence in each case.

1. A. If you had stood at home and done your homework, you would not have failed in arithmetic.
   B. Her affected manner annoyed every member of the audience.
   C. How will the new law affect our income taxes?
   D. The plants were not affected by the long, cold winter, but they succumbed to the drought of summer.

   1.____

2. A. He is one of the most able men who have been in the Senate.
   B. It is he who is to blame for the lamentable mistake.
   C. Haven't you a helpful suggestion to make at this time?
   D. The money was robbed from the blind man's cup.

   2.____

3. A. The amount of children in this school is steadily increasing.
   B. After taking an apple from the table, she went out to play.
   C. He borrowed a dollar from me.
   D. I had hoped my brother would arrive before me.

   3.____

4. A. Whom do you think I hear from every week?
   B. Who do you think is the right man for the job?
   C. Who do you think I found in the room?
   D. He is the man whom we considered a good candidate for the presidency.

   4.____

5. A. Quietly the puppy laid down before the fireplace.
   B. You have made your bed; now lie in it.
   C. I was badly sunburned because I had lain too long in the sun.
   D. I laid the doll on the bed and left the room.

   5.____

KEY (CORRECT ANSWERS)

1. A
2. D
3. A
4. C
5. A

PREPARING WRITTEN MATERIAL

PARAGRAPH REARRANGEMENT
COMMENTARY

The sentences that follow are in scrambled order. You are to rearrange them in proper order and indicate the letter choice containing the correct answer at the space at the right.

Each group of sentences in this section is actually a paragraph presented in scrambled order. Each sentence in the group has a place in that paragraph; no sentence is to be left out. You are to read each group of sentences and decide upon the best order in which to put the sentences so as to form a well-organized paragraph.

The questions in this section measure the ability to solve a problem when all the facts relevant to its solution are not given.

More specifically, certain positions of responsibility and authority require the employee to discover connection between events sometimes, apparently, unrelated. In order to do this, the employee will find it necessary to correctly infer that unspecified events have probably occurred or are likely to occur. This ability becomes especially important when action must be taken on incomplete information.

Accordingly, these questions require competitors to choose among several suggested alternatives, each of which presents a different sequential arrangement of the events. Competitors must choose the MOST logical of the suggested sequences.

In order to do so, they may be required to draw on general knowledge to infer missing concepts or events that are essential to sequencing the given events. Competitors should be careful to infer only what is essential to the sequence. The plausibility of the wrong alternatives will always require the inclusion of unlikely events or of additional chains of events which are NOT essential to sequencing the given events.

It's very important to remember that you are looking for the best of the four possible choices, and that the best choice of all may not even be one of the answers you're given to choose from.

There is no one right way to solve these problems. Many people have found it helpful to first write out the order of the sentences, as they would have arranged them, on their scrap paper before looking at the possible answers. If their optimum answer is there, this can save them some time. If it isn't, this method can still give insight into solving the problem. Others find it most helpful to just go through each of the possible choices, contrasting each as they go along. You should use whatever method feels comfortable and works for you.

While most of these types of questions are not that difficult, we've added a higher percentage of the difficult type, just to give you more practice. Usually there are only one or two questions on this section that contain such subtle distinctions that you're unable to answer confidently. And you then may find yourself stuck deciding between two possible choices, neither of which you're sure about.

EXAMINATION SECTION

TEST 1

DIRECTIONS: The following groups of sentences need to be arranged in an order that makes sense. Select the letter preceding the sequence that represents the BEST sentence order. *PRINT THE LETTER OF THE CORRECT ANSWER IN THE SPACE AT THE RIGHT.*

1.
   I. The keyboard was purposely designed to be a little awkward to slow typists down.
   II. The arrangement of letters on the keyboard of a typewriter was not designed for the convenience of the typist.
   III. Fortunately, no one is suggesting that a new keyboard be designed right away.
   IV. If one were, we would have to learn to type all over again.
   V. The reason was that the early machines were slower than the typists and would jam easily.
   The CORRECT answer is:
   A. I, III, IV, II, V
   B. II, V, I, IV, III
   C. V, I, II, III, IV
   D. II, I, V, III, IV

1.____

2.
   I. The majority of the new service jobs are part-time or low-paying.
   II. According to the U.S. Bureau of Labor Statistics, jobs in the service sector constitute 72% of all jobs in this country.
   III. If more and more workers receive less and less money, who will buy the goods and services needed to keep the economy going?
   IV. The service sector is by far the fastest growing part of the United States economy.
   V. Some economists look upon this trend with great concern.
   The CORRECT answer is:
   A. II, IV, I, V, III
   B. II, III, IV, I, V
   C. V, IV, II, III, I
   D. III, I, II, IV, V

2.____

3.
   I. They can also affect one's endurance.
   II. This can stabilize blood sugar levels, and ensure that the brain is receiving a steady, constant, supply of glucose, so that one is *hitting on all cylinders* while taking the test.
   III. By food, we mean real food, not junk food or unhealthy snacks.
   IV. For this reason, it is important not to skip a meal, and to bring food with you to the exam.
   V. One's blood sugar levels can affect how clearly one is able to think and concentrate during an exam.
   The CORRECT answer is:
   A. V, IV, II, III, I
   B. V, II, I, IV, III
   C. V, I, IV, III, II
   D. V, IV, I, III, II

3.____

4. I. Those who are the embodiment of desire are absorbed in material quests, and those who are the embodiment of feeling are warriors who value power more than possession.
    II. These qualities are in everyone, but in different degrees.
    III. But those who value understanding yearn not for goods or victory, but for knowledge.
    IV. According to Plato, human behavior flows from three main sources: desire, emotion, and knowledge.
    V. In the perfect state, the industrial forces would produce but not rule, the military would protect but not rule, and the forces of knowledge, the philosopher kings, would reign.
    The CORRECT answer is:
    A. IV, V, I, II, III
    B. V, I, II, III, IV
    C. IV, III, II, I, V
    D. IV, II, I, III, V

5. I. Of the more than 26,000 tons of garbage produced daily in New York City, 12,000 tons arrive daily at Fresh Kills.
    II. In a month, enough garbage accumulates there to fill the Empire State Building.
    III. In 1937, the Supreme Court halted the practice of dumping the trash of New York City into the sea.
    IV. Although the garbage is compacted, in a few years the mounds of garbage at Fresh Kills will be the highest points south of Maine's Mount Desert Island on the Eastern Seaboard.
    V. Instead, tugboats now pull barges of much of the trash to Staten Island and the largest landfill in the world, Fresh Kills.
    The CORRECT answer is:
    A. III, V, IV, I, II
    B. III, V, II, IV, I
    C. III, V, I, II, IV
    D. III, II, V, IV, I

6. I. Communists rank equality very high, but freedom very low.
    II. Unlike communists, conservatives place a high value on freedom and a very low value on equality.
    III. A recent study demonstrated that one way to classify people's political beliefs is to look at the importance placed on two words: freedom and equality.
    IV. Thus, by demonstrating how members of these groups feel about the two words, the study has proved to be useful for political analysts in several European countries.
    V. According to the study, socialists and liberals rank both freedom and equality very high, while fascists rate both very low.
    The CORRECT answer is:
    A. III, V, I, II, IV
    B. V, IV, III, I, II
    C. III, V, IV, II, I
    D. III, I, II, IV, V

7. I. "Can there be anything more amazing than this?"
    II. If the riddle is successfully answered, his dead brothers will be brought back to life.
    III. "Even though man sees those around him dying every day," says Dharmaraj, "he still believes and acts as if he were immortal."
    IV. "What is the cause of ceaseless wonder?" asks the Lord of the Lake.
    V. In the ancient epic, The Mahabharata, a riddle is asked of one of the Pandava brothers.
    The CORRECT answer is:
    A. V, II, I, IV, III
    B. V, IV, III, I, II
    C. V, II, IV, III, I
    D. V, II, IV, I, III

8. I. On the contrary, the two main theories—the cooperative (neoclassical) theory and the radical (labor theory)—clearly rest on very different assumptions, which have very different ethical overtones.
    II. The distribution of income is the primary factor in determining the relative levels of material well-being that different groups or individuals attain.
    III. Of all issues in economics, the distribution of income is one of the most controversial.
    IV. The neoclassical theory tends to support the existing income distribution (or minor changes), while the labor theory ends to support substantial changes in the way income is distributed.
    V. The intensity of the controversy reflects the fact that different economic theories are not purely neutral, *detached* theories with no ethical or moral implications.
    The CORRECT answer is:
    A. II, I, V, IV, III
    B. III, II, V, I, IV
    C. III, V, II, I, IV
    D. III, V, IV, I, II

9. I. The pool acts as a broker and ensures that the cheapest power gets used first.
    II. Every six seconds, the pool's computer monitors all of the generating stations in the state and decides which to ask for more power and which to cut back.
    III. The buying and selling of electrical power is handled by the New York Power Pool in Guilderland, New York.
    IV. This is to the advantage of both the buying and selling utilities.
    V. The pool began operation in 1970, and consists of the state's eight electric utilities.
    The CORRECT answer is:
    A. V, I, II, III, IV
    B. IV, II, I, III, V
    C. III, V, I, IV, II
    D. V, III, IV, II, I

10. I. Modern English is much simpler grammatically than Old English.
    II. Finnish grammar is very complicated; there are some fifteen cases, for example.
    III. Chinese, a very old language, may seem to be the exception, but it is the great number of characters/words that must be mastered that makes it so difficult to learn, not its grammar.
    IV. The newest literary language—that is, written as well as spoken—is Finish, whose literary roots go back only to about the middle of the nineteenth century.
    V. Contrary to popular belief, the longer a language is been in use the simpler its grammar—not the reverse.
    The CORRECT answer is:
    A. IV, I, II, III, V
    B. V, I, IV, II, III
    C. I, II, IV, III, V
    D. IV, II, III, I, V

KEY (CORRECT ANSWERS)

1.	D	6.	A
2.	A	7.	C
3.	C	8.	B
4.	D	9.	C
5.	C	10.	B

TEST 2

DIRECTIONS: This type of question tests your ability to recognize accurate paraphrasing, well-constructed paragraphs, and appropriate style and tone. It is important that the answer you select contains only the facts or concepts given in the original sentences. It is also important that you be aware of incomplete sentences, inappropriate transitions, unsupported opinions, incorrect usage, and illogical sentence order. Paragraphs that do not include all the necessary facts and concepts, that distort them, or that add new ones are not considered correct.

The format for this section may vary. Sometimes, long paragraphs are given, and emphasis is placed on style and organization. Our first five questions are of this type. Other times, the paragraphs are shorter, and there is less emphasis on style and more emphasis on accurate representation of information. Our second group of five questions are of this nature.

For each of Questions 1 through 10, select the paragraph that BEST expresses the ideas contained in the sentences above it. *PRINT THE LETTER OF THE CORRECT ANSWER IN THE SPACE AT THE RIGHT.*

1. I. Listening skills are very important for managers.   1.____
    II. Listening skills are not usually emphasized.
    III. Whenever managers are depicted in books, manuals or the media, they are always talking, never listening.
    IV. We'd like you to read the enclosed handout on listening skills and to try to consciously apply them this week.
    V. We guarantee they will improve the quality of your interactions.

    A. Unfortunately, listening skills are not usually emphasized for managers. Managers are always depicted as talking, never listening. We'd like you to read the enclosed handout on listening skills. Please try to apply these principles this week. If you do, we guarantee they will improve the quality of your interactions.
    B. The enclosed handout on listening skills will be important improving the quality of your interactions. We guarantee it. All you have to do is take sometime this week to read and to consciously try to apply the principles. Listening skills are very important for manages, but they are not usually emphasized. Whenever managers are depicted in books, manuals or the media, they are always talking, never listening.
    C. Listening well is one of the most important skills a manager can have, yet it's not usually given much attention. Think about any representation of managers in books, manuals, or in the media that you may have seen. They're always talking, never listening. We'd like you to read the enclosed handout on listening skills and consciously try to apply them the rest of the week. We guarantee you will see a difference in the quality of your interactions.

123

D. Effective listening, one very important tool in the effective manager's arsenal, is usually not emphasized enough. The usual depiction of managers in books, manuals or the media is one in which they are always talking, never listening. We'd like you to read the enclosed handout and consciously try to apply the information contained therein throughout the rest of the week. We feel sure that you will see a marked difference in the quality of your interactions.

2.
I. Chekhov wrote three dramatic masterpieces which share certain themes and formats: Uncle Vanya, The Cherry Orchard, and The Three Sisters.
II. They are primarily concerned with the passage of time and how this erodes human aspirations.
III. The plays are haunted by the ghosts of the wasted life.
IV. The characters are concerned with life's lesser problems; however, such as the inability to make decisions, loyalty to the wrong cause, and the inability to be clear.
V. This results in sweet, almost aching, type of a sadness referred to as Chekhovian.

2.____

A. Chekhov wrote three dramatic masterpieces: Uncle Vanya, The Cherry Orchard, and The Three Sisters. These masterpieces share certain themes and formats: the passage of time, how time erodes human aspirations, and the ghosts of wasted life. Each masterpiece is characterized by a sweet, almost aching, type of sadness that has become known as Chekhovian. The sweetness of this sadness hinges on the fact that it is not the great tragedies of life which are destroying these characters, but their minor flaws: indecisiveness, misplaced loyalty, unclarity.
B. The Cherry Orchard, Uncle Vanya, and The Three Sisters are three dramatic masterpieces written by Chekhov that use similar formats to explore a common theme. Each is primarily concerned with the way that passing time wears down human aspirations, and each is haunted by the ghosts of the wasted life. The characters are shown struggling futilely with the lesser problems of life: indecisiveness, loyalty to the wrong cause, and the inability to be clear. These struggles create a mood of sweet, almost aching, sadness that has become known as Chekhovian.
C. Chekhov's dramatic masterpieces are, along with The Cherry Orchard, Uncle Vanya, and The Three Sisters. These plays share certain thematic and formal similarities. They are concerned most of all with the passage of time and the way in which time erodes human aspirations. Each play is haunted by the specter of the wasted life. Chekhov's characters are caught, however, by life's lesser snares: indecisiveness, loyalty to the wrong cause, and unclarity. The characteristic mood is a sweet, almost aching type of sadness that has come to be known as Chekhovian.
D. A Chekhovian mood is characterized by sweet, almost aching, sadness. The term comes from three dramatic tragedies by Chekhov which revolve around the sadness of a wasted life. The three masterpieces (Uncle Vanya, The Three Sisters, and The Cherry Orchard) share the same

theme and format. The plays are concerned with how the passage of time erodes human aspirations. They are peopled with characters who are struggling with life's lesser problems. These are people who are indecisive, loyal to the wrong causes, or are unable to make themselves clear.

3.
I. Movie previews have often helped producers decide which parts of movies they should take out or leave in.
II. The first 1933 preview of King Kong was very helpful to the producers because many people ran screaming from the theater and would not return when four men first attacked by Kong were eaten by giant spiders.
III. The 1950 premiere of Sunset Boulevard resulted in the filming of an entirely new beginning, and a delay of six months in the film's release.
IV. In the original opening scene, William Holden was in a morgue talking with thirty-six other "corpses" about the ways some of them had died.
V. When he began to tell them of his life with Gloria Swanson, the audience found this hilarious, instead of taking the scene seriously.

3._____

A. Movie previews have often helped producers decide what parts of movies they should leave in or take out. For example, the first preview of King Kong in 1933 was very helpful. In one scene, four men were first attacked by Kong and then eaten by giant spiders. Many members of the audience ran screaming from the theater and would not return. The premiere of the 1950 film Sunset Boulevard was also very helpful. In the original opening scene, William Holden was in a morgue with thirty-six other "corpses," discussing the ways some of them had died. When he began to tell them of his life with Gloria Swanson, the audience found this hilarious. They were supposed to take the scene seriously. The result was a delay of six months in the release of the film while a new beginning was added.

B. Movie previews have often helped producers decide whether they should change various parts of a movie. After the 1933 preview of King Kong, a scene in which four men who had been attacked by Kong were eaten by giant spiders was taken out as many people ran screaming from the theater and would not return. The 1950 premiere of Sunset Boulevard also led to some changes. In the original opening scene, William Holden was in a morgue talking with thirty-six other "corpses" about the ways some of them had died. When he began to tell them of his life with Gloria Swanson, the audience found this hilarious, instead of taking the scene seriously.

C. What do Sunset Boulevard and King Kong have in common? Both show the value of using movie previews to test audience reaction. The first 1933 preview of King Kong showed that a scene showing four men being eaten by giant spiders after having been attacked by Kong was too frightening for many people. They ran screaming from the theater and couldn't be coaxed back. The 1950 premiere of Sunset Boulevard was also a scream, but not the kind the producers intended. The movie opens with William Holden lying in a morgue discussing the ways they had died with thirty-six other "corpses." When he began to tell them of his life with Gloria Swanson, the audience couldn't take him seriously. Their laughter caused a six-month delay while the beginning was rewritten.

D. Producers very often use movie previews to decide if changes are needed. The premiere of Sunset Boulevard in 1950 led to a new beginning and a six-month delay in film release. At the beginning, William Holden and thirty-six other "corpses" discuss the ways some of them died. Rather than taking this seriously, the audience thought it was hilarious when he began to tell them of his life with Gloria Swanson. The first 1933 preview of King Kong was very helpful for its producers because one scene so terrified the audience that many of them ran screaming from the theater and would not return. In this particular scene, four men who had first been attacked by Kong were eaten by giant spiders.

4.
I. It is common for supervisors to view employees as "things" to be manipulated.
II. This approach does not motivate employees, nor does the carrot-and-stick approach because employees often recognize these behaviors and resent them.
III. Supervisors can change these behaviors by using self-inquiry and persistence.
IV. The best managers genuinely respect those they work with, are supportive and helpful, and are interested in working as a team with those they supervise.
V. They disagree with the Golden Rule that says "he or she who has the gold makes the rules."

4.____

A. Some managers act as if they think the Golden Rule means "he or she who has the gold makes the rules." They show disrespect to employees by seeing them as "things" to be manipulated. Obviously, this approach does not motivate employees any more than the carrot-and-stick approach motivates them. The employees are smart enough to spot these behaviors and resent them. On the other hand, the managers genuinely respect those they work with, are supportive and helpful, and are interested in working as a team. Self-inquiry and persistence can change even the former type of supervisor into the latter.

B. Many supervisors all into the trap of viewing employees as "things" to be manipulated, or try to motivate them by using a carrot-and-stick approach. These methods do not motivate employees, who often recognize the behaviors and resent them. Supervisors can change these behaviors, however, by using self-inquiry and persistence. The best managers are supportive and helpful, and have genuine respect for those with whom they work. They are interested in working as a team with those they supervise. To them, the Golden Rule is not "he or she who has the gold makes the rules."

C. Some supervisors see employees as "things" to be used or manipulated using a carrot-and-stick technique. These methods don't work. Employees often see through them and resent them. A supervisor who wants to change may do so. The techniques of self-inquiry and persistence can be used to turn him or her into the type of supervisor who doesn't think the Golden Rule is "he or she who has the gold makes the rules." They may become like the best managers who treat those with whom they work with respect and give them help and support. These are the manager who know how to build a team.

D. Unfortunately, many supervisors act as if their employees are objects whose movements they can position at will. This mistaken belief has the same result as another popular motivational technique—the carrot-and-stick approach. Both attitudes can lead to the same result—resentment from those employees who recognize the behaviors for what they are. Supervisors who recognize these behaviors can change through the use of persistence and the use of self-inquiry. It's important to remember that the best managers respect their employees. They readily give necessary help and support and are interested in working as a team with those they supervise. To these managers, the Golden Rule is not "he or she who has the gold makes the rules."

5.
I. The first half of the nineteenth century produced a group of pessimistic poets—Byron, De Musset, Heine, Pushkin, and Leopardi.
II. It also produced a group of pessimistic composers—Schubert, Chopin, Schumann, and even the later Beethoven.
III. Above all, in philosophy, there was the profoundly pessimistic philosopher, Schopenhauer.
IV. The Revolution was dead, the Bourbons were restored, the feudal barons were reclaiming their land, and progress everywhere was being suppressed, as the great age was over.
V. "I thank God," said Goethe, "that I am not young in so thoroughly finished a world."

5.____

A. "I thank God," said Goethe, "that I am not young in so thoroughly finished a world." The Revolution was dead, the Bourbons were restored, the feudal barons were reclaiming their land, and progress everywhere was being suppressed. The first half of the nineteenth century produced a group of pessimistic poets: Byron, De Musset, Heine, Pushkin, and Leopardi. It also produced pessimistic composers: Schubert, Chopin, Schumann. Although Beethoven came later, he fits into this group, too. Finally and above all, it also produced a profoundly pessimistic philosopher, Schopenhauer. The great age was over.

B. The first half of the nineteenth century produced a group of pessimistic poets: Byron, De Musset, Heine, Pushkin, and Leopardi. It produced a group of pessimistic composers: Schubert, Chopin, Schumann, and even the later Beethoven. Above all, it produced a profoundly pessimistic philosopher, Schopenhauer. For each of these men, the great age was over. The Revolution was dead, and the Bourbons were restored. The feudal barons were reclaiming their land, and progress everywhere was being suppressed.

C. The great age was over. The Revolution was dead—the Bourbons were restored, and the feudal barons were reclaiming their land. Progress everywhere was being suppressed. Out of this climate came a profound pessimism. Poets, like Byron, De Musset, Heine, Pushkin, and Leopardi; composers, like Schubert, Chopin, Schumann, and even the later Beethoven; and above all, a profoundly pessimistic philosopher, Schopenauer. This pessimism which arose in the first half of the nineteenth century is illustrated by these words of Goethe, "I thank God that I am not young in so thoroughly finished a world."

D. The first half of the nineteenth century produced a group of pessimistic poets, Byron, De Musset, Heine, Pushkin, and Leopardi—and a group of pessimistic composers, Schubert, Chopin, Schumann, and the later Beethoven. Above it all, it produced a profoundly pessimistic philosopher, Schopenhauer. The great age was over. The Revolution was dead, the Bourbons were restored, the feudal barons were reclaiming their land, and progress everywhere was being suppressed. "I thank God," said Goethe, "that I am not young in so thoroughly finished a world."

6.
I. A new manager sometimes may feel insecure about his or her competence in the new position.
II. The new manager may then exhibit defensive or arrogant behavior towards those one supervises, or the new manager may direct overly flattering behavior toward one's new supervisor.

6.____

A. Sometimes, a new manager may feel insecure about his or her ability to perform well in this new position. The insecurity may lead him or her to treat others differently. He or she may display arrogant or defensive behavior towards those he or she supervises, or be overly flattering to his or her new supervisor.
B. A new manager may sometimes feel insecure about his or her ability to perform well in the new position. He or she may then become arrogant, defensive, or overly flattering towards those he or she works with.
C. There are times when a new manager may be insecure about how well he or she can perform in the new job. The new manager may also behave defensive or act in an arrogant way towards those he or she supervises, or overly flatter his or her boss.
D. Sometimes a new manager may feel insecure about his or her ability to perform well in the new position. He or she may then display arrogant or defensive behavior towards those they supervise, or become overly flattering towards their supervisors.

7.
I. It is possible to eliminate unwanted behavior by bringing it under stimulus control—tying the behavior to a cue, and then never, or rarely, giving the cue.
II. One trainer successfully used this method to keep an energetic young porpoise from coming out of her tank whenever she felt like it, which was potentially dangerous.
III. Her trainer taught her to do it for a reward, in response to a hand signal, and then rarely gave the signal.

7.____

A. Unwanted behavior can be eliminated by tying the behavior to a cue, and then never, or rarely, giving the cue. This is called stimulus control. One trainer was able to use this method to keep an energetic young porpoise from coming out of her tank by teaching her to come out for a reward in response to a hand signal, and then rarely giving the signal.
B. Stimulus control can be used to eliminate unwanted behavior. In this method, behavior is tied to a cue, and then the cue is rarely, if ever, given. One trainer was able to successfully use stimulus control to keep an energetic young porpoise from coming out of her tank whenever she felt like it—a potentially dangerous practice. She taught the porpoise to come out for a reward when she gave a hand signal, and then rarely gave the signal.
C. It is possible to eliminate behavior that is undesirable by bringing it under stimulus control by tying behavior to a signal, and then rarely giving the signal. One trainer successfully used this method to keep an energetic porpoise from coming out of her tank, a potentially dangerous situation. Her trainer taught the porpoise to do it for a reward, in response to a hand signal, and then would rarely give the signal.
D. By using stimulus control, it is possible to eliminate unwanted behavior by tying the behavior to a cue, and then rarely or never give the cue. One trainer was able to use this method to successfully stop a young porpoise from coming out of her tank whenever she felt like it. To curb this potentially dangerous practice, the porpoise was taught by the trainer to come out of the tank for a reward, in response to a hand signal, and then rarely given the signal.

8. I. There is a great deal of concern over the safety of commercial trucks, caused by their greatly increased role in serious accidents since federal deregulation in 1981.
   II. Recently, 60 percent of trucks in New York and Connecticut and 70 percent of trucks in Maryland randomly stopped by state troopers failed safety inspections.
   III. Sixteen states in the United States require no training at all for truck drivers.

   A. Since federal deregulation in 1981, there has been a great deal of concern over the safety of commercial trucks, and their greatly increased role in serious accidents. Recently, 60 percent of trucks in New York and Connecticut, and 70 percent of trucks in Maryland failed safety inspections. Sixteen states in the United States require no training at all for truck drivers.
   B. There is a great deal of concern over the safety of commercial trucks since federal deregulation in 1981. Their role in serious accidents has greatly increased. Recently, 60 percent of trucks randomly stopped in Connecticut and New York and 70 percent in Maryland failed safety inspections conducted by state troopers. Sixteen states in the United States provide no training at all for truck drivers.
   C. Commercial trucks have a greatly increased role in serious accidents since federal deregulation in 1981. This has led to a great deal of concern.

8.____

8 (#2)

Recently, 70 percent of trucks in Maryland and 60 percent of trucks in New York and Connecticut failed inspection of those that were randomly stopped by state troopers. Sixteen states in the United States require no training for all truck drivers.

D. Since federal deregulation in 1981, the role that commercial trucks have played in serious accidents has greatly increased, and this has led to a great deal of concern. Recently, 60 percent of trucks in New York and Connecticut, and 70 percent of trucks in Maryland randomly stopped by state troopers failed safety inspections. Sixteen states in the U.S. don't require any training for truck drivers.

9. I. No matter how much some people have, they still feel unsatisfied and want more, or want to keep what they have forever.
   II. One recent television documentary showed several people flying from New York to Paris for a one-day shopping spree to buy platinum earrings, because they were bored.
   III. In Brazil, some people were ordering coffins that cost a minimum of $45,000 and are equipping them with deluxe stereos, televisions, and other graveyard necessities.

9.____

   A. Some people, despite having a great deal, still feel unsatisfied and want more, or think they can keep what they have forever. One recent documentary on television showed several people enroute from Paris to New York for a one day shopping spree to buy platinum earrings, because they were bored. Some people in Brazil are even ordering coffins equipped with such graveyard necessities as deluxe stereos and televisions. The price of the coffins start at $45,000.
   B. No matter how much some people have, they may feel unsatisfied. This leads them to want more, or to want to keep what they have forever. Recently, a television documentary depicting several people flying from New York to Paris for a one day shopping spree to buy platinum earrings. They were bored. Some people in Brazil are ordering coffins that cost at least $45,000 and come equipped with deluxe televisions, stereos and other necessary graveyard items.
   C. Some people will be dissatisfied no matter how much they have. They may want more, or they may want to keep what they have forever. One recent television documentary showed several people, motivated by boredom, jetting from New York to Paris for a one-day shopping spree to buy platinum earrings. In Brazil, some people are ordering coffins equipped with deluxe stereos, televisions and other graveyard necessities. The minimum price for these coffins—$45,000.
   D. Some people are never satisfied. No matter how much they have they still want more, or think they can keep what they have forever. One television documentary recently showed several people flying from New York to Paris for the day to buy platinum earrings because they were bored. In Brazil, some people are ordering coffins that cost $45,000 and are equipped with deluxe stereos, televisions and other graveyard necessities.

10.
I. A television signal or video signal has three parts.
II. Its parts are the black-and-white portion, the color portion, and the synchronizing (sync) pulses, which keep the picture stable.
III. Each video source, whether it's a camera or a video-cassette recorder contains its own generator of these synchronizing pulses to accompany the picture that it's sending in order to keep it steady and straight.
IV. In order to produce a clean recording, a video-cassette recorder must "lock-up" to the sync pulses that are part of the video it is trying to record, and this effort may be very noticeable if the device does not have gunlock.

10._____

A. There are three parts to a television or video signal: the black-and-white part, the color part, and the synchronizing (sync) pulses, which keep the picture stable. Whether it's a video-cassette recorder or a camera, each video source contains its own pulse that synchronizes and generates the picture it's sending in order to keep it straight and steady. A video-cassette recorder must "lock up" to the sync pulses that are part of the video it's trying to record. If the device doesn't have gunlock, this effort must be very noticeable.
B. A video signal or television is comprised of three parts: the black-and-white portion, the color portion, and the sync (synchronizing) pulses, which keep the picture stable. Whether it's a camera or a video-cassette recorder, each video source contains its own generator of these synchronizing pulses. These accompany the picture that it's sending in order to keep it straight and steady. A video-cassette recorder must "lock up" to the sync pulses that are part of the video it is trying to record in order to produce a clean recording. This effort may be very noticeable if the device does not have gunlock.
C. There are three parts to a television or video signal: the color portion, the black-and-white portion, and the sync (synchronizing pulses). These keep the picture stable. Each video source, whether it's a video-cassette recorder or a camera, generates these synchronizing pulses accompanying the picture it's sending in order to keep it straight and steady. If a clean recording is to be produced, a video-cassette recorder must store the sync pulses that are part of the video it is trying to record. This effort may not be noticeable if the device does not have gunlock.
D. A television signal or video signal has three parts: the black-and-white portion, the color portion, and the synchronizing (sync) pulses. It's the sync pulses which keep the picture stable, which accompany it and keep it steady and straight. Whether it's a camera or a video-cassette recorder, each video source contains its own generator of these synchronizing pulses. To produce a clean recording, a video-cassette recorder must "lock up" to the sync pulses that are part of the video it is trying to record. If the device does not have gunlock, this effort may be very noticeable.

KEY (CORRECT ANSWERS)

1. C   6. A
2. B   7. B
3. A   8. D
4. B   9. C
5. D   10. D

INTERPRETING STATISTICAL DATA
GRAPHS, CHARTS AND TABLES
EXAMINATION SECTION
TEST 1

DIRECTIONS: Each questioner incomplete statement is followed by several suggested answers or completions. Select the one that BEST answers the question or completes the statement. *PRINT THE LETTER OF THE CORRECT ANSWER IN THE SPACE AT THE RIGHT.*

Questions 1-3.

DIRECTIONS: Questions 1 through 3 are to be answered SOLELY on the basis of the following table.

QUARTERLY SALES REPORTED BY MAJOR INDUSTRY GROUPS

DECEMBER 2021 – FEBRUARY 2023
Reported Sales, Taxable & Non-Taxable (in Millions)

Industry Groups	12/21-2/22	3/22-5/22	6/22-8/22	9/22-11/22	12/22-2/23
Retailers	2,802	2,711	2,475	2,793	2,974
Wholesalers	2,404	2,237	2,269	2,485	2,974
Manufacturers	3,016	2,888	3,001	3,518	3,293
Services	1,034	1,065	984	1,132	1,092

1. The trend in total reported sales may be described as

    A. downward
    B. downward and upward
    C. horizontal
    D. upward

2. The two industry groups that reveal a similar seasonal pattern for the period December 2021 through November 2022 are

    A. retailers and manufacturers
    B. retailers and wholesalers
    C. wholesalers and manufacturers
    D. wholesalers and service

3. Reported sales were at a MINIMUM between

    A. December 2021 and February 2022
    B. March 2022 and May 2022
    C. June 2022 and August 2022
    D. September 2022 and November 2022

TEST 2

DIRECTIONS: Each question or incomplete statement is followed by several suggested answers or completions. Select the one that BEST answers the question or completes the statement. *PRINT THE LETTER OF THE CORRECT ANSWER IN THE SPACE AT THE RIGHT*

Questions 1-4.

DIRECTIONS: Questions 1 through 4 are to be answered SOLELY on the basis of the following information.

The income elasticity of demand for selected items of consumer demand in the United States are:

Item	Elasticity
Airline Travel	5.66
Alcohol	.62
Dentist Fees	1.00
Electric Utilities	3.00
Gasoline	1.29
Intercity Bus	1.89
Local Bus	1.41
Restaurant Meals	.75

1. The demand for the item listed below that would be MOST adversely affected by a decrease in income is

   A. alcohol
   B. electric utilities
   C. gasoline
   D. restaurant meals

2. The item whose relative change in demand would be the same as the relative change in income would be

   A. dentist fees
   B. gasoline
   C. restaurant meals
   D. none of the above

3. If income increases by 12 percent, the demand for restaurant meals may be expected to increase by

   A. 9 percent
   B. 12 percent
   C. 16 percent
   D. none of the above

4. On the basis of the above information, the item whose demand would be MOST adversely affected by an increase in the sales tax from 7 percent to 8 percent to be passed on to the consumer in the form of higher prices

   A. would be airline travel
   B. would be alcohol
   C. would be gasoline
   D. cannot be determined

TEST 3

DIRECTIONS: Each question or incomplete statement is followed by several suggested answers or completions. Select the one that BEST answers the question or completes the statement. *PRINT THE LETTER OF THE CORRECT ANSWER IN THE SPACE AT THE RIGHT.*

Questions 1-3.

DIRECTIONS: Questions 1 through 3 are to be answered SOLELY on the basis of the following graphs depicting various relationships in a single retail store.

GRAPH 1
RELATIONSHIP BETWEEN NUMBER OF CUSTOMERS STORE AND TIME OF DAY

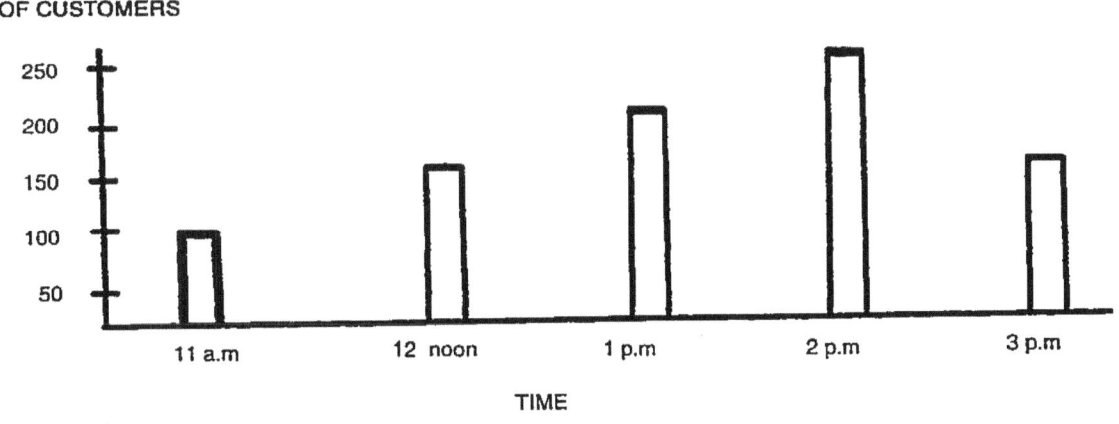

GRAPH II
RELATIONSHIP BETWEEN NUMBER OF CHECK-OUT LANES AVAILABLE IN STORE AND WAIT TIME FOR CHECK-OUT

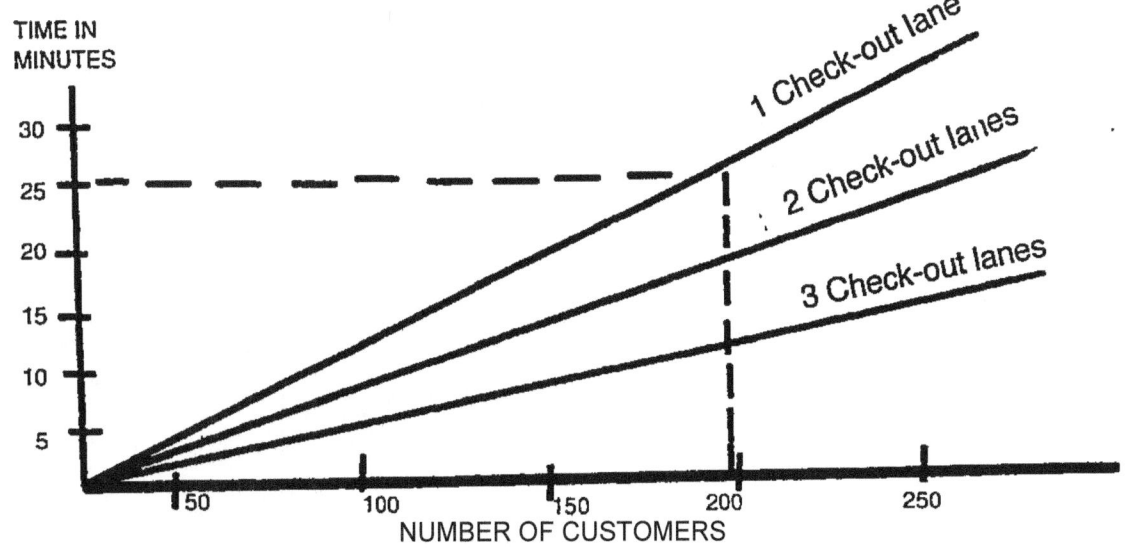

Note the dotted lines in Graph II. They demonstrate that, if there are 200 people in the store and only one check-out lane is open, the wait time will be 25 minutes.

135

1. At what time would a person be most likely NOT to have to wait more than 15 minutes if only one check-out lane is open?

    A. 11 A.M.   B. 12 Noon   C. 1 P.M.   D. 3 P.M.

2. At what time of day would a person have to wait the LONGEST to check out if three check-out lanes are available?

    A. 11 A.M.   B. 12 Noon   C. 1 P.M.   D. 2 P.M

3. The difference in wait times between 1 and 3 check-out lanes at 3 P.M. is MOST NEARLY

    A. 5   B. 10   C. 15   D. 20

TEST 4

DIRECTIONS: Each question or incomplete statement is followed by several suggested answers or completions. Select the one that BEST answers the question or completes the statement. *PRINT THE LETTER OF THE CORRECT ANSWER IN THE SPACE AT THE RIGHT.*

Questions 1-4.

DIRECTIONS: Questions 1 through 4 are to be answered SOLELY on the basis of the graph below.

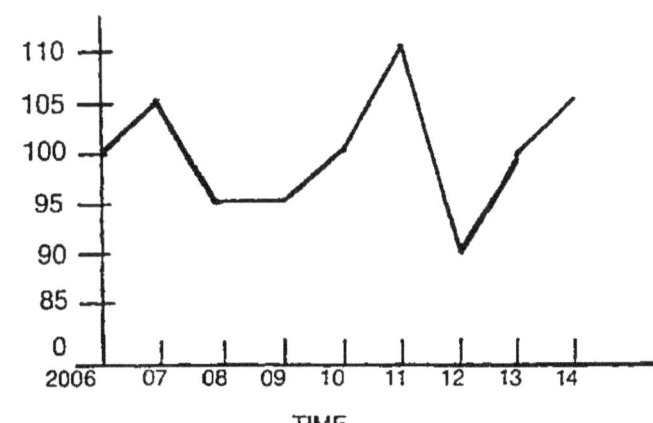

1. Of the following, during what four-year period did the average output of computer operators fall BELOW 100 sheets per hour?

    A. 2007-10   B. 2008-11   C. 2010-13   D. 2011-14

2. The average percentage change in output over the previous year's output for the years 2009 to 2012 is MOST NEARLY

    A. 2   B. 0   C. -5   D. -7

3. The difference between the actual output for 2012 and the projected figure based upon the average increase from 2006-2011 is MOST NEARLY

    A. 18   B. 20   C. 22   D. 24

4. Assume that after constructing the above graph you, an analyst, discovered that the average number of entries per sheet in 2012 was 25 (instead of 20) because of the complex nature of the work performed during that period.
   The average output in sheets per hour for the period 2010-13, expressed in terms of 20 items per sheet, would then be MOST NEARLY

    A. 95   B. 100   C. 105   D. 110

TEST 6

DIRECTIONS: Each question or incomplete statement is followed by several suggested answers or completions. Select the one that BEST answers the question or completes the statement. *PRINT THE LETTER OF THE CORRECT ANSWER IN THE SPACE AT THE RIGHT.*

Questions 1-3.

DIRECTIONS: Questions 1 through 3 are to be answered on the basis of the following data assembled for a cost-benefit analysis.

	Cost	Benefit
No program	0	0
Alternative W	$ 3,000	$ 6,000
Alternative X	$10,000	$17,000
Alternative Y	$17,000	$25,000
Alternative Z	$30,000	$32,000

1. From the point of view of selecting the alternative with the best cost benefit ratio, the BEST alternative is Alternative

   A. W   B. X   C. Y   D. Z

2. From the point of view of selecting the alternative with the best measure of net benefit, the BEST alternative is Alternative

   A. W   B. X   C. Y   D. Z

3. From the point of view of pushing public expenditure to the point where marginal benefit equals or exceeds marginal cost, the BEST alternative is Alternative

   A. W   B. X   C. Y   D. Z

TEST 6

DIRECTIONS: Each question or incomplete statement is followed by several suggested answers or completions. Select the one that BEST answers the question or completes the statement. *PRINT THE LETTER OF THE CORRECT ANSWER IN THE SPACE AT THE RIGHT.*

Questions 1-3.

DIRECTIONS: Questions 1 through 3 are to be answered SOLELY on the basis of the following data.

A series of cost-benefit studies of various alternative health programs yields the following results:

Program	Benefit	Cost
K	30	15
L	60	60
M	300	150
N	600	500

In answering Questions 1 and 2, assume that all programs can be increased or decreased in scale without affecting their individual benefit-to-cost ratios.

1. The benefit-to-cost ratio of Program M is

    A. 10:1   B. 5:1   C. 2:1   D. 1:2

2. The budget ceiling for one or more of the programs included in the study is set at 75 units. It may MOST logically be concluded that

    A. Programs K and L should be chosen to fit within the budget ceiling
    B. Program K would be the most desirable one that could be afforded
    C. Program M should be chosen rather than Program K
    D. the choice should be between Programs M and K

3. If no assumptions can be made regarding the effects of change of scale, the MOST logical conclusion, on the basis of the data available, is that

    A. more data are needed for a budget choice of program
    B. Program K is the most preferable because of its low cost and good benefit-to-cost ratio
    C. Program M is the most preferable because of its high benefits and good benefit-to-cost ratio
    D. there is no difference between Programs K and M, and either can be chosen for any purpose

TEST 7

DIRECTIONS: Each question or incomplete statement is followed by several suggested answers or completions. Select the one that BEST answers the question or completes the statement. *PRINT THE LETTER OF THE CORRECT ANSWER IN THE SPACE AT THE RIGHT.*

Questions 1-6.

DIRECTIONS: Questions 1 through 6 are to be answered SOLELY on the basis of the information contained in the charts below which relate to the budget allocations of City X, a small suburban community. The charts depict the annual budget allocations by Department and by expenditures over a five-year period.

CITY X BUDGET IN MILLIONS OF DOLLARS
TABLE I. Budget Allocations by Department

Department	2017	2018	2019	2020	2021
Public Safety	30	45	50	40	50
Health and Welfare	50	75	90	60	70
Engineering	5	8	10	5	8
Human Resources	10	12	20	10	22
Conservation & Environment	10	15	20	20	15
Education & Development	15	25	35	15	15
TOTAL BUDGET	120	180	225	150	180

TABLE II. Budget Allocations by Expenditures

Category	2017	2018	2019	2020	2021
Raw Materials & Machinery	36	63	68	30	98
Capital Outlay	12	27	56	15	18
Personal Services	72	90	101	105	64
TOTAL BUDGET	120	180	225	150	180

1. The year in which the SMALLEST percentage of the total annual budget was allocated to the Department of Education and Development is

   A. 2017   B. 2018   C. 2020   D. 2021

2. Assume that in 2020 the Department of Conservation and Environment divided its annual budget into the three categories of expenditures and in exactly the same proportion as the budget shown in Table II for the year 2020. The amount allocated for capital outlay in the Department of Conservation and Environment's 2020 budget was MOST NEARLY _____ million.

   A. $2   B. $4   C. $6   D. $10

3. From the year 2018 to the year 2020, the sum of the annual budgets for the Departments of Public Safety and Engineering showed an overall _____ million.

   A. decline; SB
   B. increase; $7
   C. decline; S15
   D. increase; S22

4. The LARGEST dollar increase in departmental budget allocations from one year to the next was in _____ from _____.

   A. Public Safety; 2017 to 2018
   B. Health and Welfare; 2017 to 2018
   C. Education and Development; 2019 to 2020
   D. Human Resources; 2019 to 2020

5. During the five-year period, the annual budget of the Department of Human Resources was GREATER than the annual budget for the Department of Conservation and Environment in _____ of the years.

   A. none   B. one   C. two   D. three

6. If the total City X budget increases at the same rate from 2021 to 2022 as it did from 2020 to 2021, the total City X budget for 2022 will be MOST NEARLY _____ million.

   A. $180   B. $200   C. $210   D. $215

TEST 8

DIRECTIONS: Each question or incomplete statement is followed by several suggested answers or completions. Select the one that BEST answers the question or completes the statement. *PRINT THE LETTER OF THE CORRECT ANSWER IN THE SPACE AT THE RIGHT.*

Questions 1-3.

DIRECTIONS: Questions 1 through 3 are to be answered SOLELY on the basis of the following information.

Assume that in order to encourage Program A, the State and Federal governments have agreed to make the following reimbursements for money spent on Program A, provided the unreimbursed balance is paid from City funds.

During Fiscal Year 2021-2022 - For the first $2 million expended, 50% Federal reimbursement and 30% State reimbursement; for the next $3 million, 40% Federal reimbursement and 20% State reimbursement; for the next $5 million, 20% Federal reimbursement and 10% State reimbursement. Above $10 million expended, no Federal or State reimbursement.

During Fiscal Year 2022-2023 - For the first $1 million expended, 30% Federal reimbursement and 20% State reimbursement; for the next $4 million, 15% Federal reimbursement and 10% State reimbursement. Above $5 million expended, no Federal or State reimbursement.

1. Assume that the Program A expenditures are such that the State reimbursement for Fiscal Year 2021-2022 will be $1 million.
   Then, the Federal reimbursement for Fiscal Year 2021-2022 will be

   A. $1,600,000 B. $1,800,000
   C. $2,000,000 D. $2,600,000

2. Assume that $8 million were to be spent on Program A in Fiscal Year 2022-2023.
   The TOTAL amount of unreimbursed City funds required would be

   A. $3,500,000 B. $4,500,000
   C. $5,500,000 D. $6,500,000

3. Assume that the City desires to have a combined total of $6 million spent in Program A during both the Fiscal Year 2021-2022 and the Fiscal Year 2022-2023.
   Of the following expenditure combinations, the one which results in the GREATEST reimbursement of City funds is _____ in Fiscal Year 2021-2022 and _____ in Fiscal Year 2022-2023.

   A. $5 million; $1 million B. $4 million; $2 million
   C. $3 million; $3 million D. $2 million; $4 million

KEY (CORRECT ANSWERS)

TEST 1

1. D
2. C
3. C

TEST 2

1. B
2. A
3. A
4. D

TEST 3

1. A
2. D
3. B

TEST 4

1. A
2. B
3. C
4. C

TEST 5

1. A
2. C
3. C

TEST 6

1. C
2. D
3. A

TEST 7

1. D
2. A
3. A
4. B
5. B
6. D

TEST 8

1. B
2. D
3. A

PRINCIPLES AND PRACTICES, OF ADMINISTRATION, SUPERVISION AND MANAGEMENT

TABLE OF CONTENTS

	Page
GENERAL ADMINISTRATION	1
SEVEN BASIC FUNCTIONS OF THE SUPERVISOR	2
I. Planning	2
II. Organizing	3
III. Staffing	3
IV. Directing	3
V. Coordinating	3
VI. Reporting	3
VII. Budgeting	3
PLANNING TO MEET MANAGEMENT GOALS	4
I. What is Planning	4
II. Who Should Make Plans	4
III. What are the Results of Poor Planning	4
IV. Principles of Planning	4
MANAGEMENT PRINCIPLES	5
I. Management	5
II. Management Principles	5
III. Organization Structure	6
ORGANIZATION	8
I. Unity of Command	8
II. Span of Control	8
III. Uniformity of Assignment	9
IV. Assignment of Responsibility and Delegation of Authority	9
PRINCIPLES OF ORGANIZATION	9
I. Definition	9
II. Purpose of Organization	9
III. Basic Considerations in Organizational Planning	9
IV. Bases for Organization	10
V. Assignment of Functions	10
VI. Delegation of Authority and Responsibility	10
VII. Employee Relationships	11

DELEGATING		11
I.	WHAT IS DELEGATING:	11
II.	TO WHOM TO DELEGATE	11
REPORTS		12
I.	DEFINITION	12
II.	PURPOSE	12
III.	TYPES	12
IV.	FACTORS TO CONSIDER BEFORE WRITING REPORT	12
V.	PREPARATORY STEPS	12
VI.	OUTLINE FOR A RECOMMENDATION REPORT	12
MANAGEMENT CONTROLS		13
I.	Control	13
II.	Basis for Control	13
III.	Policy	13
IV.	Procedure	14
V.	Basis of Control	14
FRAMEWORK OF MANAGEMENT		14
I.	Elements	14
II.	Manager's Responsibility	15
III.	Control Techniques	16
IV.	Where Forecasts Fit	16
PROBLEM SOLVING		16
I.	Identify the Problem	16
II.	Gather Data	17
III.	List Possible Solutions	17
IV.	Test Possible Solutions	18
V.	Select the Best Solution	18
VI.	Put the Solution into Actual Practice	19
COMMUNICATION		19
I.	What is Communication?	19
II.	Why is Communication Needed?	19
III.	How is Communication Achieved?	20
IV.	Why Does Communication Fail?	21
V.	How to Improve Communication	21
VI.	How to Determine If You Are Getting Across	21
VII.	The Key Attitude	22
HOW ORDERS AND INSTRUCTIONS SHOULD BE GIVEN		22
I.	Characteristics of Good Orders and Instructions	22
FUNCTIONS OF A DEPARTMENT PERSONNEL OFFICE		23

SUPERVISION	23
I. Leadership	23
A. The Authoritarian Approach	23
B. The Laissez-Faire Approach	24
C. The Democratic Approach	24
II. Nine Points of Contrast Between Boss and Leader	25
EMPLOYEE MORALE	25
I. Some Ways to Develop and Maintain Good Employee Morale	25
II. Some Indicators of Good Morale	26
MOTIVATION	26
EMPLOYEE PARTICIPATION	27
I. WHAT IS PARTICIPATION	27
II. WHY IS IT IMPORTANT?	27
III. HOW MAY SUPERVISORS OBTAIN IT?	28
STEPS IN HANDLING A GRIEVANCE	28
DISCIPLINE	29
I. THE DISCIPLINARY INTERVIEW	29
II. PLANNING THE INTERVIEW	29
III. CONDUCTING THE INTERVIEW	30

PRINCIPLES AND PRACTICES, OF
ADMINISTRATION, SUPERVISION AND MANAGEMENT

Most people are inclined to think of administration as something that only a few persons are responsible for in a large organization. Perhaps this is true if you are thinking of Administration with a capital A, but administration with a lower case *a* is a responsibility of supervisors at all levels each working day.

All of us feel we are pretty good supervisors and that we do a good job of administering the workings of our agency. By and large, this is true, but every so often it is good to check up on ourselves. Checklists appear from time to time in various publications which psychologists say tell whether or not a person will make a good wife, husband, doctor, lawyer, or supervisor.

The following questions are an excellent checklist to test yourself as a supervisor and administrator.

Remember, Administration gives direction and points the way but administration carries the ideas to fruition. Each is dependent on the other for its success. Remember, too, that no unit is too small for these departmental functions to be carried out. These statements apply equally as well to the Chief Librarian as to the Department Head with but one or two persons to supervise.

GENERAL ADMINISTRATION: General Responsibilities of Supervisors

1. Have I prepared written statements of functions, activities, and duties for my organizational unit?

2. Have I prepared procedural guides for operating activities?

3. Have I established clearly in writing, lines of authority and responsibility for my organizational unit?

4. Do I make recommendations for improvements in organization, policies, administrative and operating routines and procedures, including simplification of work and elimination of non-essential operations?

5. Have I designated and trained an understudy to function in my absence?

6. Do I supervise and train personnel within the unit to effectively perform their assignments?

7. Do I assign personnel and distribute work on such a basis as to carry out the organizational unit's assignment or mission in the most effective and efficient manner?

8. Have I established administrative controls by:

    a. Fixing responsibility and accountability on all supervisors under my direction for the proper performance of their functions and duties.

b. Preparations and submitting periodic work load and progress reports covering the operations of the unit to my immediate superior.

c. Analysis and evaluation of such reports received from subordinate units.

d. Submission of significant developments and problems arising within the organizational unit to my immediate superior.

e. Conducting conferences, inspections, etc., as to the status and efficiency of unit operations.

9. Do I maintain an adequate and competent working force?

10. Have I fostered good employee-department relations, seeing that established rules, regulations, and instructions are being carried out properly?

11. Do I collaborate and consult with other organizational units performing related functions to insure harmonious and efficient working relationships?

12. Do I maintain liaison through prescribed channels with city departments and other governmental agencies concerned with the activities of the unit?

13. Do I maintain contact with and keep abreast of the latest developments and techniques of administration (professional societies, groups, periodicals, etc.) as to their applicability to the activities of the unit?

14. Do I communicate with superiors and subordinates through prescribed organizational channels?

15. Do I notify superiors and subordinates in instances where bypassing is necessary as soon thereafter as practicable?

16. Do I keep my superior informed of significant developments and problems?

SEVEN BASIC FUNCTIONS OF THE SUPERVISOR

I. PLANNING
This means working out goals and means to obtain goals. <u>What</u> needs to be done, <u>who</u> will do it, <u>how</u>, <u>when</u>, and <u>where</u> it is to be done.

SEVEN STEPS IN PLANNING

A. Define job or problem clearly.
B. Consider priority of job.
C. Consider time-limit—starting and completing.
D. Consider minimum distraction to, or interference with, other activities.
E. Consider and provide for contingencies—possible emergencies.
F. Break job down into components.

G. Consider the 5 W's and H:
   WHY..........is it necessary to do the job? (Is the purpose clearly defined?)
   WHAT........needs to be done to accomplish the defined purpose?
   ....is needed to do the job? (Money, materials, etc.)
   WHO..........is needed to do the job?
   ....will have responsibilities?
   WHERE......is the work to be done?
   WHEN........is the job to begin and end? (Schedules, etc.)
   HOW..........is the job to bed done? (Methods, controls, records, etc.)

II. ORGANIZING

This means dividing up the work, establishing clear lines of responsibility and authority and coordinating efforts to get the job done.

III. STAFFING

The whole personnel function of bringing in and <u>training</u> staff, getting the right man and fitting him to the right job—the job to which he is best suited.

In the normal situation, the supervisor's responsibility regarding staffing normally includes providing accurate job descriptions, that is, duties of the jobs, requirements, education and experience, skills, physical, etc.; assigning the work for maximum use of skills; and proper utilization of the probationary period to weed out unsatisfactory employees.

IV. DIRECTING

Providing the necessary leadership to the group supervised. Important work gets done to the supervisor's satisfaction.

V. COORDINATING

The all-important duty of inter-relating the various parts of the work.
The supervisor is also responsible for controlling the coordinated activities. This means measuring performance according to a time schedule and setting quotas to see that the goals previously set are being reached. Reports from workers should be analyzed, evaluated, and made part of all future plans.

VI. REPORTING

This means proper and effective communication to your superiors, subordinates, and your peers (in definition of the job of the supervisor). Reports should be read and information contained therein should be used, not be filed away and forgotten. Reports should be written in such a way that the desired action recommended by the report is forthcoming.

VII. BUDGETING
This means controlling current costs and forecasting future costs. This forecast is based on past experience, future plans and programs, as well as current costs.

You will note that these seven functions can fall under three topics:

Planning) Make a plan Organizing)	Staffing) Directing) Get things done Controlling)	Reporting) Watch it work Budgeting)

PLANNING TO MEET MANAGEMENT GOALS

I. WHAT IS PLANNING?

   A. Thinking a job through before new work is done to determine the best way to do it
   B. A method of doing something
   C. Ways and means for achieving set goals
   D. A means of enabling a supervisor to deliver with a minimum of effort, all details involved in coordinating his work

II. WHO SHOULD MAKE PLANS?

   Everybody!
   All levels of supervision must plan work. (Top management, heads of divisions or bureaus, first line supervisors, and individual employees.) The higher the level, the more planning required.

III. WHAT ARE THE RESULTS OF POOR PLANNING?

   A. Failure to meet deadline
   B. Low employee morale
   C. Lack of job coordination
   D. Overtime is frequently necessary
   E. Excessive cost, waste of material and manhours

IV. PRINCIPLES OF PLANNING

   A. Getting a clear picture of your objectives. What exactly are you trying to accomplish?
   B. Plan the whole job, then the parts, in proper sequence.
   C. Delegate the planning of details to those responsible for executing them.
   D. Make your plan flexible.
   E. Coordinate your plan with the plans of others so that the work may be processed with a minimum of delay.
   F. Sell your plan before you execute it.
   G. Sell your plan to your superior, subordinate, in order to gain maximum participation and coordination.
   H. Your plan should take precedence. Use knowledge and skills that others have brought to a similar job.
   I. Your plan should take account of future contingencies; allow for future expansion.
   J. Plans should include minor details. Leave nothing to chance that can be anticipated.
   K. Your plan should be simple and provide standards and controls. Establish quality and quantity standards and set a standard method of doing the job. The controls will indicate whether the job is proceeding according to plan.
   L. Consider possible bottlenecks, breakdowns, or other difficulties that are likely to arise.

V. Q. WHAT ARE THE YARDSTICKS BY WHICH PLANNING SHOULD BE MEASURED?
A. Any plan should:
— Clearly state a definite course of action to be followed and goal to be achieved, with consideration for emergencies.
— Be realistic and practical.
— State what's to be done, when it's to be done, where, how, and by whom.
— Establish the most efficient sequence of operating steps so that more is accomplished in less time, with the least effort, and with the best quality results.
— Assure meeting deliveries without delays.
— Establish the standard by which performance is to be judged.

Q. WHAT KINDS OF PLANS DOES EFFECTIVE SUPERVISION REQUIRE?
A. Plans should cover such factors as:
— Manpower: right number of properly trained employees on the job
— Materials: adequate supply of the right materials and supplies
— Machines: full utilization of machines and equipment, with proper maintenance
— Methods: most efficient handling of operations
— Deliveries: making deliveries on time
— Tools: sufficient well-conditioned tools
— Layout: most effective use of space
— Reports: maintaining proper records and reports
— Supervision: planning work for employees and organizing supervisor's own time

MANAGEMENT PRINCIPLES

I. MANAGEMENT
Q. What do we mean by management?
A. Getting work done through others.

Management could also be defined as planning, directing, and controlling the operations of a bureau or division so that all factors will function properly and all persons cooperate efficiently for a common objective.

II. MANAGEMENT PRINCIPLES

A. There should be a hierarchy—wherein authority and responsibility run upward and downward through several levels—with a broad base at the bottom and a single head at the top.

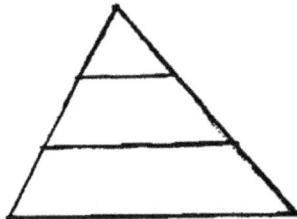

B. Each and every unit or person in the organization should be answerable ultimately to the manager at the apex. In other words, *The buck stops here!*

C. Every necessary function involved in the bureau's objectives is assigned to a unit in that bureau.

D. Responsibilities assigned to a unit are specifically clear-cut and understood.

E. Consistent methods of organizational structure should be applied at each level of the organization.

F. Each member of the bureau from top to bottom knows: to whom he reports and who reports to him.

G. No member of one bureau reports to more than one supervisor. No dual functions.

H. Responsibility for a function is matched by authority necessary to perform that function. Weight of authority.

I. Individuals or units reporting to a supervisor do not exceed the number which can be feasibly and effectively coordinated and directed. Concept of *span of control*.

J. Channels of command (management) are not violated by staff units, although there should be staff services to facilitate and coordinate management functions.

K. Authority and responsibility should be decentralized to units and individuals who are responsible for the actual performance of operations.
Welfare – down to Welfare Centers
Hospitals – down to local hospitals

L. Management should exercise control through attention to policy problems of exceptional performance, rather than through review of routine actions of subordinates.

M. Organizations should never be permitted to grow so elaborate as to hinder work accomplishments.

III. ORGANIZATION STRUCTURE

Types of Organizations
The purest form is a leader and a few followers, such as:

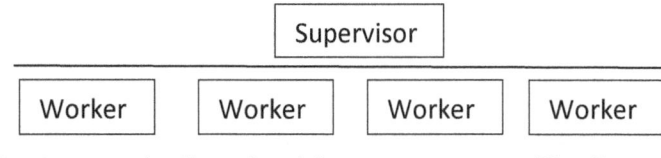

(Refer to organization chart) from supervisor to workers.

The line of authority is direct, The workers know exactly where they stand in relation to their boss, to whom they report for instructions and direction.

Unfortunately, in our present complex society, few organizations are similar to this example of a pure line organization. In this era of specialization, other people are often needed in the simplest of organizations. These specialists are known as staff. The sole purpose for their existence (staff) is to assist, advise, suggest, help or counsel line organizations. Staff has no authority to direct line people—nor do they give them direct instructions.

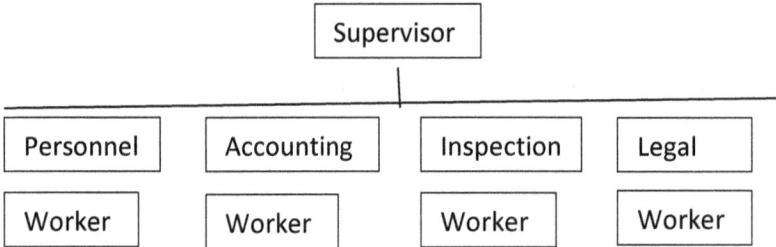

Line Functions
1. Directs
2. Orders
3. Responsibility for carrying out activities from beginning to end
4. Follows chain of command
5. Is identified with what it does
6. Decides when and how to use staff advice
7. Line executes

Staff Functions
1. Advises
2. Persuades and sells
3. Staff studies, reports, recommends but does not carry out
4. May advise across department lines
5. May find its ideas identified with others
6. Has to persuade line to want its advice

7. Staff: Conducts studies and research. Provides advice and instructions in technical matters. Serves as technical specialist to render specific services.

Types and Functions of Organization Charts
An organization chart is a picture of the arrangement and inter-relationship of the subdivisions of an organization.

A. Types of Charts:
   1. Structural: basic relationships only
   2. Functional: includes functions or duties
   3. Personnel: positions, salaries, status, etc.
   4. Process Chart: work performed
   5. Gantt Chart: actual performance against planned
   5. Flow Chart: flow and distribution of work

B. Functions of Charts:
   1. Assist in management planning and control
   2. Indicate duplication of functions
   3. Indicate incorrect stressing of functions
   4. Indicate neglect of important functions
   5. Correct unclear authority
   6. Establish proper span of control

C. Limitations of Charts:
   1. Seldom maintained on current basis
   2. Chart is oversimplified
   3. Human factors cannot adequately be charted

D. Organization Charts should be:
   1. Simple
   2. Symmetrical
   3. Indicate authority
   4. Line and staff relationship differentiated
   5. Chart should be dated and bear signature of approving officer
   6. Chart should be displayed, not hidden

ORGANIZATION

There are four basic principles of organization:
1. Unity of command
2. Span of control
3. Uniformity of assignment
4. Assignment of responsibility and delegation of authority

I. UNITY OF COMMAND

Unity of command means that each person in the organization should receive orders from one, and only one, supervisor. When a person has to take orders from two or more people, (a) the orders may be in conflict and the employee is upset because he does not know which he should obey, or (b) different orders may reach him at the same time and he does not know which he should carry out first.

Equally as bad as having two bosses is the situation where the supervisor is bypassed. Let us suppose you are a supervisor whose boss bypasses you (deals directly with people reporting to you). To the worker, it is the same as having two bosses; but to you, the supervisor, it is equally serious. Bypassing on the part of your boss will undermine your authority, and the people under you will begin looking to your boss for decisions and even for routine orders.

You can prevent bypassing by telling the people you supervise that if anyone tries to give them orders, they should direct that person to you.

II. SPAN OF CONTROL

Span of control on a given level involves:
A. The number of people being supervised
B. The distance
C The time involved in supervising the people. (One supervisor cannot supervise too many workers effectively.)

Span of control means that a supervisor has the right number (not too many and not too few) of subordinates that he can supervise well.

III. UNIFORMITY OF ASSIGNMENT

In assigning work, you as the supervisor should assign to each person jobs that are similar in nature. An employee who is assigned too many different types of jobs will waste time in going from one kind of work to another. It takes time for him to get to top production in one kind of task and, before he does so, he has to start on another.
When you assign work to people, remember that:

A. Job duties should be definite. Make it clear from the beginning <u>what</u> they are to do, <u>how</u> they are to do it, and <u>why</u> they are to do it. Let them know how much they are expected to do and how well they are expected to do it.
B. Check your assignments to be certain that there are no workers with too many unrelated duties, and that no two people have been given overlapping responsibilities. Your aim should be to have every task assigned to a specific person with the work fairly distributed and with each person doing his part.

IV. ASSIGNMENT OF RESPONSIBILITY AND DELEGATION OF AUTHORITY

A supervisor cannot delegate his final responsibility for the work of his department. The experienced supervisor knows that he gets his work done through people. He can't do it all himself. So he must assign the work and the responsibility for the work to his employees. Then they must be given the authority to carry out their responsibilities.

By assigning responsibility and delegating authority to carry out the responsibility, the supervisor builds in his workers initiative, resourcefulness, enthusiasm, and interest in their work. He is treating them as responsible adults. They can find satisfaction in their work, and they will respect the supervisor and be loyal to the supervisor.

PRINCIPLES OF ORGANIZATION

I. DEFINITION

Organization is the method of dividing up the work to provide the best channels for coordinated effort to get the agency's mission accomplished.

II. PURPOSE OF ORGANIZATION

A. To enable each employee within the organization to clearly know his responsibilities and relationships to his fellow employees and to organizational units
B. To avoid conflicts of authority and overlapping of jurisdiction.
C. To ensure teamwork.

III. BASIC CONSIDERATIONS IIN ORGANIZATIONAL PLANNING

A. The basic plans and objectives of the agency should be determined, and the organizational structure should be adapted to carry out effectively such plans and objectives.
B. The organization should be built around the major functions of the agency and not individuals or groups of individuals.

C. The organization should be sufficiently flexible to meet new and changing conditions which may be brought about from within or outside the department.
D. The organizational structure should be as simple as possible and the number of organizational units kept at a minimum.
E. The number of levels of authority should be kept at a minimum. Each additional management level lengthens the chain of authority and responsibility and increases the time for instructions to be distributed to operating levels and for decisions to be obtained from higher authority.
F. The form of organization should permit each executive to exercise maximum initiative within the limits of delegated authority.

IV. BASES FOR ORGANIZATION

A. Purpose (Examples: education, police, sanitation)
B. Process (Examples: accounting, legal, purchasing)
C. Clientele (Examples: welfare, parks, veteran)
D. Geographic (Examples: borough offices, precincts, libraries)

V. ASSIGNMENTS OF FUNCTIONS

A. Every function of the agency should be assigned to a specific organizational unit. Under normal circumstances, no single function should be assigned to more than one organizational unit.
B. There should be no overlapping, duplication, or conflict between organizational elements.
C. Line functions should be separated from staff functions, and proper emphasis should be placed on staff activities.
D. Functions which are closely related or similar should normally be assigned to a single organizational unit.
E. Functions should be properly distributed to promote balance, and to avoid overemphasis of less important functions and underemphasis of more essential functions.

VI. DELEGATION OF AUTHORITY AND RESPONSIBILITY

A. Responsibilities assigned to a specific individual or organizational unit should carry corresponding authority, and all statements of authority or limitations thereof should be as specific as possible.
B. Authority and responsibility for action should be decentralized to organizational units and individuals responsible for actual performance to the greatest extent possible, without relaxing necessary control over policy or the standardization of procedures. Delegation of authority will be consistent with decentralization of responsibility but such delegation will not divest an executive in higher authority of his overall responsibility.
C. The heads of organizational units should concern themselves with important matters and should delegate to the maximum extent details and routines performed in the ordinary course of business.
D. All responsibilities, authorities, and relationships should be stated in simple language to avoid misinterpretation.
E. Each individual or organizational unit charged with a specific responsibility will be held responsible for results.

VII. EMPLOYEE RELATIONSHIPS

   A. The employees reporting to one executive should not exceed the number which can be effectively directed and coordinated. The number will depend largely upon the scope and extent of the responsibilities of the subordinates.
   B. No person should report to more than one supervisor. Every supervisor should know who reports to him, and every employee should know to whom he reports. Channels of authority and responsibility should not be violated by staff units.
   C. Relationships between organizational units within the agency and with outside organizations and associations should be clearly stated and thoroughly understood to avoid misunderstanding.

DELEGATING

I. WHAT IS DELEGATING?
Delegating is assigning a job to an employee, giving him the authority to get that job done, and giving him the responsibility for seeing to it that the job is done.

   A. What To Delegate
      1. Routine details
      2. Jobs which may be necessary and take a lot of time, but do not have to be done by the supervisor personally (preparing reports, attending meetings, etc.)
      3. Routine decision-making (making decisions which do not require the supervisor's personal attention)

   B. What Not To Delegate
      1. Job details which are *executive functions* (setting goals, organizing employees into a good team, analyzing results so as to plan for the future)
      2. Disciplinary power (handling grievances, preparing service ratings, reprimands, etc.)
      3. Decision-making which involves large numbers of employees or other bureaus and departments
      4. Final and complete responsibility for the job done by the unit being supervised

   C. Why Delegate?
      1. To strengthen the organization by developing a greater number of skilled employees
      2. To improve the employee's performance by giving him the chance to learn more about the job, handle some responsibility, and become more interested in getting the job done
      3. To improve a supervisor's performance by relieving him of routine jobs and giving him more time for *executive functions* (planning, organizing, controlling, etc.) which cannot be delegated

II. TO WHOM TO DELEGATE
People with abilities not being used. Selection should be based on ability, not on favoritism.

REPORTS

I. **DEFINITION**
A report is an orderly presentation of factual information directed to a specific reader for a specific purpose

II. **PURPOSE**
The general purpose of a report is to bring to the reader useful and factual information about a condition or a problem. Some specific purposes of a report may be:

A. To enable the reader to appraise the efficiency or effectiveness of a person or an operation
B. To provide a basis for establishing standards
C. To reflect the results of expenditures of time, effort, and money
D. To provide a basis for developing or altering programs

III. **TYPES**

A. Information Report: Contains facts arranged in sequence
B. Summary (Examination) Report: Contains facts plus an analysis or discussion of the significance of the facts. Analysis may give advantages and disadvantages or give qualitative and quantitative comparisons
C. Recommendation Report: Contains facts, analysis, and conclusion logically drawn from the facts and analysis, plus a recommendation based upon the facts, analysis, and conclusions

IV. **FACTORS TO CONSIDER BEFORE WRITING REPORT**

A. <u>Why</u> write the report?: The purpose of the report should be clearly defined.
B. <u>Who</u> will read the report?: What level of language should be used? Will the reader understand professional or technical language?
C. <u>What</u> should be said?: What does the reader need or want to know about the subject?
D. <u>How</u> should it be said?: Should the subject be presented tactfully? Convincingly? In a stimulating manner?

V. **PREPARATORY STEPS**

A. Assemble the facts: Find out who, why, what, where, when, and how.
B. Organize the facts: Eliminate unnecessary information
C. Prepare an outline: Check for orderliness, logical sequence
D. Prepare a draft: Check for correctness, clearness, completeness, conciseness, and tone
E. Prepare it in final form: Check for grammar, punctuation, appearance

VI. **OUTLINE FOR A RECOMMENDATION REPORT**

Is the report:
A. Correct in information, grammar, and tone?
B. Clear?
C. Complete?

D. Concise?
E. Timely?
F. Worth its cost?

Will the report accomplish its purpose?

MANAGEMENT CONTROLS

I. CONTROL
What is control? What is controlled? Who controls?

The essence of control is action which adjusts operations to predetermined standards, and its basis is information in the hands of managers. Control is checking to determine whether plans are being observed and suitable progress toward stated objectives is being made, and action is taken, if necessary, to correct deviations.

We have a ready-made model for this concept of control in the automatic systems which are widely used for process control in the chemical land petroleum industries. A process control system works this way. Suppose, for example, it is desired to maintain a constant rate of flow of oil through a pipe at a predetermined or set-point value. A signal, whose strength represents the rate of flow, can be produced in a measuring device and transmitted to a control mechanism. The control mechanism, when it detects any deviation of the actual from the set-point signal, will reposition the value regulating flow rate.

II. BASIS FOR CONTROL

A process control mechanism thus acts to adjust operations to predetermined standards and does so on the basis of information it receives. In a parallel way, information reaching a manager gives him the opportunity for corrective action and is his basis for control. He cannot exercise control without such information, and he cannot do a complete job of managing without controlling.

III. POLICY

What is policy?

Policy is simply a statement of an organization's intention to act in certain ways when specified types of circumstances arise. It represents a general decision, predetermined and expressed as a principle or rule, establishing a normal pattern of conduct for dealing with given types of business events—usually recurrent. A statement is therefore useful in economizing the time of managers and in assisting them to discharge their responsibilities equitably and consistently.

Policy is not a means of control, but policy does generate the need for control.

Adherence to policies is not guaranteed nor can it be taken on faith. It has to be verified. Without verification, there is no basis for control. Policy and procedures, although closely related and interdependent to a certain extent, are not synonymous. A policy may be adopted, for example, to maintain a materials inventory not to exceed one million dollars.

A procedure for inventory control could interpret that policy and convert it into methods for keeping within that limit, with consideration, too, of possible but foreseeable expedient deviation.

IV. PROCEDURE

What is procedure?

A procedure specifically prescribes:
A. What work is to be performed by the various participants
B. Who are the respective participants
C. When and where the various steps in the different processes are to be performed
D. The sequence of operations that will insure uniform handling of recurring transactions
E. The paper that is involved, its origin, transition, and disposition

Necessary appurtenances to a procedure are:
A. Detailed organizational chart
B. Flow charts
C. Exhibits of forms, all presented in close proximity to the text of the procedure

V. BASIS OF CONTROL – INFORMATION IN THE HANDS OF MANAGERS

If the basis of control is information in the hands of managers, then reporting is elevated to a level of very considerable importance.

Types of reporting may include:
A. Special reports and routine reports
B. Written, oral, and graphic reports
C. Staff meetings
D. Conferences
E. Television screens
F. Non-receipt of information, as where management is by exception
G. Any other means whereby information is transmitted to a manager as a basis for control action

FRAMEWORK OF MANAGEMENT

I. ELEMENTS

A. Policy: It has to be verified, controlled.

B. Organization is part of the giving of an assignment. The organizational chart gives to each individual in his title, a first approximation of the nature of his assignment and orients him as being accountable to a certain individual. Organization is not in a true sense a means of control. Control is checking to ascertain whether the assignment is executed as intended and acting on the basis of that information.

C. Budgets perform three functions:
1. They present the objectives, plans, and programs of the organization in financial terms.

2. They report the progress of actual performance against these predetermined objectives, plans, and programs.
3. Like organizational charts, delegations of authority, procedures, and job descriptions, they define the assignments which have flowed from the Chief Executive. Budgets are a means of control in the respect that they report progress of actual performance against the program. They provide information which enables managers to take action directed toward bringing actual results into conformity with the program.

D. Internal Check provides in practice for the principle that the same person should not have responsibility for all phases of a transaction. This makes it clearly an aspect of organization rather than of control. Internal Check is static, or built-in.

E. Plans, Programs, Objectives
People must know what they are trying to do. Objectives fulfill this need. Without them, people may work industriously and yet, working aimlessly, accomplish little. Plans and Programs complement Objectives, since they propose how and according to what time schedule the objectives are to be reached.

F. Delegations of Authority
Among the ways we have for supplementing the titles and lines of authority of an organizational chart are delegations of authority. Delegations of authority clarify the extent of authority of individuals and in that way serve to define assignments. That they are not means of control is apparent from the very fact that wherever there has been a delegation of authority, the need for control increases. This could hardly be expected to happen if delegations of authority were themselves means of control.

II. MANAGER'S RESPONSIBILITY

Control becomes necessary whenever a manager delegates authority to a subordinate because he cannot delegate and then simply sit back and forget4 about it. A manager's accountability to his own superior has not diminished one whit as a result of delegating part of his authority to a subordinate. The manager must exercise control over actions taken under the authority so delegated. That means checking serves as a basis for possible corrective action.

Objectives, plans, programs, organizational charts, and other elements of the managerial system are not fruitfully regarded as either controls or means of control. They are pre-established standards or models of performance to which operations are adjusted by the exercise of management control. These standards or models of performance are dynamic in character for they are constantly altered, modified, or revised. Policies, organizational set-up, procedures, delegations, etc. are constantly altered but, like objectives and plans, they remain in force until they are either abandoned or revised. All of the elements (or standards or models of performance), objectives, plans, and programs, policies, organization, etc. can be regarded as a *framework of management*.

III. CONTROL TECHNIQUES

Examples of control techniques:
A. Compare against established standards
B. Compare with a similar operation
C. Compare with past operations
D. Compare with predictions of accomplishment

IV. WHERE FORECASTS FIT

Control is after-the-fact while forecasts are before. Forecasts and projections are important for setting objectives and formulating plans.

Information for aiming and planning does not have to be before-the-fact. It may be an after-the-fact analysis proving that a certain policy has been impolitic in its effect on the relation of the company or department with customer, employee, taxpayer, or stockholder; or that a certain plan is no longer practical, or that a certain procedure is unworkable.

The prescription here certainly would not be in control (in these cases, control would simply bring operations into conformity with obsolete standards) but the establishment of new standards, a new policy, a new plan, and a new procedure to be controlled too.

Information is, of course, the basis for all communication in addition to furnishing evidence to management of the need for reconstructing the framework of management.

PROBLEM SOLVING

The accepted concept in modern management for problem solving is the utilization of the following steps:

A. Identify the problem
B. Gather data
C. List possible solutions
D. Test possible solutions
E. Select the best solution
F. Put the solution into actual practice

Occasions might arise where you would have to apply the second step of gathering data before completing the first step.

You might also find that it will be necessary to work on several steps at the same time.

I. IDENTIFY THE PROBLEM

Your first step is to define as precisely as possible the problem to be solved. While this may sound easy, it is often the most difficult part of the process.

It has been said of problem solving that you are halfway to the solution when you can write out a clear statement of the problem itself.

Our job now is to get below the surface manifestations of the trouble and pinpoint the problem. This is usually accomplished by a logical analysis, by going from the general to the particular; from the obvious to the not-so-obvious cause.

Let us say that production is behind schedule. WHY? Absenteeism is high. Now, is absenteeism the basic problem to be tackled, or is it merely a symptom of low morale among the workforce? Under these circumstances, you may decide that production is not the problem; the problem is *employee morale*.

In trying to define the problem, remember there is seldom one simple reason why production is lagging, or reports are late, etc.

Analysis usually leads to the discovery that an apparent problem is really made up of several subproblems which must be attacked separately.

Another way is to limit the problem, and thereby ease the task of finding a solution, and concentrate on the elements which are within the scope of your control.

When you have gone this far, write out a tentative statement of the problem to be solved.

II. GATHER DATA

In the second step, you must set out to collect all the information that might have a bearing on the problem. Do not settle for an assumption when reasonable fact and figures are available.

If you merely go through the motions of problem-solving, you will probably shortcut the information-gathering step. Therefore, do not stack the evidence by confining your research to your own preconceived ideas.

As you collect facts, organize them in some form that helps you make sense of them and spot possible relationships between them. For example, plotting cost per unit figures on a graph can be more meaningful than a long column of figures.

Evaluate each item as you go along. Is the source material absolutely, reliable, probably reliable, or not to be trusted.

One of the best methods for gathering data is to go out and look the situation over carefully. Talk to the people on the job who are most affected by this problem.

Always keep in mind that a primary source is usually better than a secondary source of information.

III. LIST POSSIBLE SOLUTIONS

This is the creative thinking step of problem solving. This is a good time to bring into play whatever techniques of group dynamics the agency or bureau might have developed for a joint attack on problems.

Now the important thing for you to do is: Keep an open mind. Let your imagination roam freely over the facts you have collected. Jot down every possible solution that occurs to you. Resist the temptation to evaluate various proposals as you go along. List seemingly absurd ideas along with more plausible ones. The more possibilities you list during this step, the less risk you will run of settling for merely a workable, rather than the best, solution.

Keep studying the data as long as there seems to be any chance of deriving additional ideas, solutions, explanations, or patterns from it.

IV. TEST POSSIBLE SOLUTIONS

Now you begin to evaluate the possible solutions. Take pains to be objective. Up to this point, you have suspended judgment but you might be tempted to select a solution you secretly favored all along and proclaim it as the best of the lot.

The secret of objectivity in this phase is to test the possible solutions separately, measuring each against a common yardstick. To make this yardstick try to enumerate as many specific criteria as you can think of. Criteria are best phrased as questions which you ask of each possible solution. They can be drawn from these general categories:

Suitability –	Will this solution do the job?
	Will it solve the problem completely or partially?
	Is it a permanent or a stopgap solution?
Feasibility -	Will this plan work in actual practice?
	Can we afford this approach?
	How much will it cost?
Acceptability -	Will the boss go along with the changes required in the plan?
	Are we trying to drive a tack with a sledge hammer?

V. SELECT THE BEST SOLUTION

This is the area of executive decision.

Occasionally, one clearly superior solution will stand out at the conclusion of the testing process. But often it is not that simple. You may find that no one solution has come through all the tests with flying colors.

You may also find that a proposal, which flunked miserably on one of the essential tests, racked up a very high score on others.

The best solution frequently will turn out to be a combination.

Try to arrange a marriage that will bring together the strong points of one possible solution with the particular virtues of another. The more skill and imagination that you apply, the greater is the likelihood that you will come out with a solution that is not merely adequate and workable, but is the best possible under the circumstances.

VI. PUT THE SOLUTION INTO ACTUAL PRACTICE

As every executive knows, a plan which works perfectly on paper may develop all sorts of bugs when put into actual practice.

Problem-solving does not stop with selecting the solution which looks best in theory. The next step is to put the chosen solution into action and watch the results. The results may point towards modifications.

If the problem disappears when you put your solution into effect, you know you have the right solution.

If it does not disappear, even after you have adjusted your plan to cover unforeseen difficulties that turned up in practice, work your way back through the problem-solving solutions.

> Would one of them have worked better?
> Did you overlook some vital piece of data which would have given you a different slant on the whole situation? Did you apply all necessary criteria in testing solutions? If no light dawns after this much rechecking, it is a pretty good bet that you defined the problem incorrectly in the first place.

You came up with the wrong solution because you tackled the wrong problem.

Thus, step six may become step one of a new problem-solving cycle.

COMMUNICATION

I. WHAT IS COMMUNICATION?
We communicate through writing, speaking, action, or inaction. In speaking to people face-to-face, there is opportunity to judge reactions and to adjust the message. This makes the supervisory chain one of the most, and in many instances the most, important channels of communication.

In an organization, communication means keeping employees informed about the organization's objectives, policies, problems, and progress. Communication is the free interchange of information, ideas, and desirable attitudes between and among employees and between employees and management.

II. WHY IS COMMUNICATION NEEDED?

A. People have certain social needs
B. Good communication is essential in meeting those social needs
C. While people have similar basic needs, at the same time they differ from each other
D. Communication must be adapted to these individual differences

An employee cannot do his best work unless he knows why he is doing it. If he has the feeling that he is being kept in the dark about what is going on, his enthusiasm and productivity suffer.

Effective communication is needed in an organization so that employees will understand what the organization is trying to accomplish; and how the work of one unit contributes to or affects the work of other units in the organization and other organizations.

III. HOW IS COMMUNICATION ACHIEVED?

Communication flows downward, upward, sideways.

A. Communication may come from top management down to employees. This is downward communication.

Some means of downward communication are:
1. Training (orientation, job instruction, supervision, public relations, etc.)
2. Conferences
3. Staff meetings
4. Policy statements
5. Bulletins
6. Newsletters
7. Memoranda
8. Circulation of important letters

In downward communication, it is important that employees be informed in advance of changes that will affect them.

B. Communications should also be developed so that the ideas, suggestions, and knowledge of employees will flow upward to top management.

Some means of upward communication are:
1. Personal discussion conferences
2. Committees
3. Memoranda
4. Employees suggestion program
5. Questionnaires to be filled in giving comments and suggestions about proposed actions that will affect field operations.

Upward communication requires that management be willing to listen, to accept, and to make changes when good ideas are present. Upward communication succeeds when there is no fear of punishment for speaking out or lack of interest at the top. Employees will share their knowledge and ideas with management when interest is shown and recognition is given.

C. The advantages of downward communication:
1. It enables the passing down of orders, policies, and plans necessary to the continued operation of the station.
2. By making information available, it diminishes the fears and suspicions which result from misinformation and misunderstanding.
3. It fosters the pride people want to have in their work when they are told of good work.
4. It improves the morale and stature of the individual to be *in the know*.

5. It helps employees to understand, accept, and cooperate with changes when they know about them in advance.

D. The advantages of upward communication:
1. It enables the passing upward of information, attitudes, and feelings.
2. It makes it easier to find out how ready people are to receive downward communication.
3. It reveals the degree to which the downward communication is understood and accepted.
4. It helps to satisfy the basic social needs.
5. It stimulates employees to participate in the operation of their organization.
6. It encourage employees to contribute ideas for improving the efficiency and economy of operations.
7. It helps to solve problem situations before they reach the explosion point.

IV. WHY DOES COMMUNICATION FAIL?

A. The technical difficulties of conveying information clearly
B. The emotional content of communication which prevents complete transmission
C. The fact that there is a difference between what management needs to say, what it wants to day, and what it does say
D. The fact that there is a difference between what employees would like to say, what they think is profitable or safe to say, and what they do say

V. HOW TO IMPROVE COMMUNICATION

As a supervisor, you are a key figure in communication. To improve as a communicator, you should:
A. Know: Knowing your subordinates will help you to recognize and work with individual differences.
B. Like: If you like those who work for you and those for whom you work, this will foster the kind of friendly, warm, work atmosphere that will facilitate communication.
C. Trust: Showing a sincere desire to communicate will help to develop the mutual trust and confidence which are essential to the free flow of communication.
D. Tell: Tell your subordinates and superiors *what's doing*. Tell your subordinates *why* as well as *how*.
E. Listen: By listening, you help others to talk and you create good listeners. Don't forget that listening implies action.
F. Stimulate: Communication has to be stimulated and encouraged. Be receptive to ideas and suggestions and motivate your people so that each member of the team identifies himself with the job at hand.
G. Consult: The most effective way of consulting is to let your people participate, insofar as possible, in developing determinations which affect them or their work.

VI. HOW TO DETERMINE WHETHER YOU ARE GETTING ACROSS

A. Check to see that communication is received and understood
B. Judge this understanding by actions rather than words
C. Adapt or vary communication, when necessary
D. Remember that good communication cannot cure all problems

VII. THE KEY ATTITUDE

Try to see things from the other person's point of view. By doing this, you help to develop the permissive atmosphere and the shared confidence and understanding which are essential to effective two-way communication.

Communication is a two-way process:
A. The basic purpose of any communication is to get action.
B. The only way to get action is through acceptance.
C. In order to get acceptance, communication must be humanly satisfying as well as technically efficient.

HOW ORDERS AND INSTRUCTIONS SHOULD BE GIVEN

I. CHARACTERISTICS OF GOOD ORDERS AND INSTRUCTIONS

   A. Clear
      Orders should be definite as to
      —What is to be done
      —Who is to do it
      —When it is to be done
      —Where it is to be done
      —How it is to be done

   B. Concise
      Avoid wordiness. Orders should be brief and to the point.

   C. Timely
      Instructions and orders should be sent out at the proper time and not too long in advance of expected performance.

   D. Possibility of Performance
      Orders should be feasible:
      1. Investigate before giving orders
      2. Consult those who are to carry out instructions before formulating and issuing them

   E. Properly Directed
      Give the orders to the people concerned. Do not send orders to people who are not concerned. People who continually receive instructions that are not applicable to them get in the habit of neglecting instructions generally.

   F. Reviewed Before Issuance
      Orders should be reviewed before issuance:
      1. Test them by putting yourself in the position of the recipient
      2. If they involve new procedures, have the persons who are to do the work review them for suggestions.

   G. Reviewed After Issuance
      Persons who receive orders should be allowed to raise questions and to point out unforeseen consequences of orders.

H. Coordinated
Orders should be coordinated so that work runs smoothly.

I. Courteous
Make a request rather than a demand. There is no need to continually call attention to the fact that you are the boss.

J. Recognizable as an Order
Be sure that the order is recognizable as such.

K. Complete
Be sure recipient has knowledge and experience sufficient to carry out order. Give illustrations and examples.

A DEPARTMENTAL PERSONNEL OFFICE IS RESPONSIBLE FOR THE FOLLOWING FUNCTIONS

1. Policy
2. Personnel Programs
3. Recruitment and Placement
4. Position Classification
5. Salary and Wage Administration
6. Employee performance Standards and Evaluation
7. Employee Relations
8. Disciplinary Actions and Separations
9. Health and Safety
10. Staff Training and Development
11. Personnel Records, Procedures, and Reports
12. Employee Services
13. Personnel Research

SUPERVISION

I. LEADERSHIP

All leadership is based essentially on authority. This comes from two sources: It is received from higher management or it is earned by the supervisor through his methods of supervision. Although effective leadership has always depended upon the leader's using his authority in such a way as to appeal successfully to the motives of the people supervised, the conditions for making this appeal are continually changing. The key to today's problem of leadership is flexibility and resourcefulness on the part of the leader in meeting changes in conditions as they occur.

Three basic approaches to leadership are generally recognized:

A. The Authoritarian Approach
1. The methods and techniques used in this approach emphasize the / in leadership and depend primarily on the formal authority of the leader. This authority is sometimes exercised in a hardboiled manner and sometimes in a benevolent

manner, but in either case the dominating role of the leader is reflected in the thinking, planning, and decisions of the group.
2. Group results are to a large degree dependent on close supervision by the leader. Usually, the individuals in the group will not show a high degree of initiative or acceptance of responsibility and their capacity to grow and develop probably will not be fully utilized. The group may react with resentment or submission, depending upon the manner and skill of the leader in using his authority.
3. This approach develops as a natural outgrowth of the authority that goes with the leader's job and his feeling of sole responsibility for getting the job done. It is relatively easy to use and does not require must resourcefulness.
4. The use of this approach is effective in times of emergencies, in meeting close deadline as a final resort, in settling some issues, in disciplinary matters, and with dependent individuals and groups.

B. The Laissez-Faire or Let 'em Alone Approach
1. This approach generally is characterized by an avoidance of leadership responsibility by the leader. The activities of the group depend largely on the choice of its members rather than the leader.
2. Group results probably will be poor. Generally, there will be disagreements over petty things, bickering, and confusion. Except for a few aggressive people, individuals will not show much initiative and growth and development will be retarded. There may be a tendency for informal leaders to take over leadership of the group.
3. This approach frequently results from the leader's dislike of responsibility, from his lack of confidence, from failure of other methods to work, from disappointment or criticism. It is usually the easiest of the three to use and requires both understanding and resourcefulness on the part of the leader.
4. This approach is occasionally useful and effective, particularly in forcing dependent individuals or groups to rely on themselves, to give someone a chance to save face by clearing his own difficulties, or when action should be delayed temporarily for good cause.

C. The Democratic Approach
1. The methods and techniques used in this approach emphasize the *we* in leadership and build up the responsibility of the group to attain its objectives. Reliance is placed largely on the earned authority of the leader.
2. Group results are likely to be good because most of the job motives of the people will be satisfied. Cooperation and teamwork, initiative, acceptance of responsibility, and the individual's capacity for growth probably will show a high degree of development.
3. This approach grows out of a desire or necessity of the leader to find ways to appeal effectively to the motivation of his group. It is the best approach to build up inside the person a strong desire to cooperate and apply himself to the job. It is the most difficult to develop, and requires both understanding and resourcefulness on the part of the leader.
4. The value of this approach increases over a long period where sustained efficiency and development of people are important. It may not be fully effective in all situations, however, particularly when there is not sufficient time to use it properly or where quick decisions must be made.

All three approaches are used by most leaders and have a place in supervising people. The extent of their use varies with individual leaders, with some using one approach predominantly. The leader who uses these three approaches, and varies their use with time and circumstance, is probably the most effective. Leadership which is used predominantly with a democratic approach requires more resourcefulness on the part of the leader but offers the greatest possibilities in terms of teamwork and cooperation.

The one best way of developing democratic leadership is to provide a real sense of participation on the part of the group, since this satisfies most of the chief job motives. Although there are many ways of providing participation, consulting as frequently as possible with individuals and groups on things that affect them seems to offer the most in building cooperation and responsibility. Consultation takes different forms, but it is most constructive when people feel they are actually helping in finding the answers to the problems on the job.

There are some requirements of leaders in respect to human relations which should be considered in their selection and development. Generally, the leader should be interested in working with other people, emotionally stable, self-confident, and sensitive to the reactions of others. In addition, his viewpoint should be one of getting the job done through people who work cooperatively in response to his leadership. He should have a knowledge of individual and group behavior, but, most important of all, he should work to combine all of these requirements into a definite, practical skill in leadership.

II. NINE POINTS OF CONTRAST BETWEEN *BOSS* AND *LEADER*

   A. The boss drives his men; the leader coaches them.
   B. The boss depends on authority; the leader on good will.
   C. The boss inspires fear; the leader inspires enthusiasm.
   D. The boss says I; the leader says *We*.
   E. The boss says *Get here on time*; the leader gets there ahead of time.
   F. The boss fixes the blame for the breakdown; the leader fixes the breakdown.
   G. The boss knows how it is done; the leader shows how.
   H. The boss makes work a drudgery; the leader makes work a game.
   I. The boss says *Go*; the leader says *Let's go*.

EMPLOYEE MORALE

Employee morale is the way employees feel about each other, the organization or unit in which they work, and the work they perform.

I. SOME WAYS TO DEVELOP AND MAINTAIN GOOD EMPLYEE MORALE

   A. Give adequate credit and praise when due.
   B. Recognize importance of all jobs and equalize load with proper assignments, always giving consideration to personality differences and abilities.
   C. Welcome suggestions and do not have an *all-wise* attitude. Request employees' assistance in solving problems and use assistants when conducting group meetings on certain subjects.
   D. Properly assign responsibilities and give adequate authority for fulfillment of such assignments.

E. Keep employees informed about matters that affect them.
F. Criticize and reprimand employees privately.
G. Be accessible and willing to listen.
H. Be fair.
I. Be alert to detect training possibilities so that you will not miss an opportunity to help each employee do a better job, and if possible with less effort on his part.
J. Set a good example.
K. Apply the golden rule.

II. SOME INDICATIONS OF GOOD MORALE

A. Good quality of work
B. Good quantity
C. Good attitude of employees
D. Good discipline
E. Teamwork
F. Good attendance
G. Employee participation

MOTIVATION

DRIVES

A drive, stated simply, is a desire or force which causes a person to do or say certain things. These are some of the most usual drives and some of their identifying characteristics recognizable in people motivated by such drives:

A. Security (desire to provide for the future)
   Always on time for work
   Works for the same employer for many years
   Never takes unnecessary chances
   Seldom resists doing what he is told

B. Recognition (desire to be rewarded for accomplishment)
   Likes to be asked for his opinion
   Becomes very disturbed when he makes a mistake
   Does things to attract attention
   Likes to see his name in print

C. Position (desire to hold certain status in relation to others)
   Boasts about important people he knows
   Wants to be known as a key man
   Likes titles
   Demands respect
   Belongs to clubs, for prestige

D. Accomplishment (desire to get things done)
   Complains when things are held up
   Likes to do things that have tangible results
   Never lies down on the job
   Is proud of turning out good work

E. Companionship (desire to associate with other people)
   Likes to work with others
   Tells stories and jokes
   Indulges in horseplay
   Finds excuses to talk to others on the job

F. Possession (desire to collect and hoard objects)
   Likes to collect things
   Puts his name on things belonging to him
   Insists on the same location

Supervisors may find that identifying the drives of employees is a helpful step toward motivating them to self-improvement and better job performance. For example: An employee's job performance is below average. His supervisor, having previously determined that the employee is motivated by a drive for security, suggests that taking training courses will help the employee to improve, advance, and earn more money. Since earning more money can be a step toward greater security, the employee's drive for security would motivate him to take the training suggested by the supervisor. In essence, this is the process of charting an employee's future course by using his motivating drives to positive advantage.

EMPLOYEE PARTICIPATION

I. WHAT IS PARTICIPATION

Employee participation is the employee's giving freely of his time, skill, and knowledge to an extent which cannot be obtained by demand.

II. WHY IS IT IMPORTANT?

The supervisor's responsibility is to get the job done through people. A good supervisor gets the job done through people who work willingly and well. The participation of employees is important because:

A. Employees develop a greater sense of responsibility when they share in working out operating plans and goals.
B. Participation provides greater opportunity and stimulation for employees to learn, and to develop their ability.
C. Participation sometimes provides better solutions to problems because such solutions may combine the experience and knowledge of interested employees who want the solutions to work.
D. An employee or group may offer a solution which the supervisor might hesitate to make for fear of demanding too much.

E. Since the group wants to make the solution work, they exert pressure in a constructive way on each other.
F. Participation usually results in reducing the need for close supervision.

II. HOW MAY SUPERVISORS OBTAIN IT?

Participation is encouraged when employees feel that they share some responsibility for the work and that their ideas are sincerely wanted and valued. Some ways of obtaining employee participation are:

A. Conduct orientation programs for new employees to inform them about the organization and their rights and responsibilities as employees.
B. Explain the aims and objectives of the agency. On a continuing basis, be sure that the employees know what these aims and objectives are.
C. Share job successes and responsibilities and give credit for success.
D. Consult with employees, both as individuals and in groups, about things that affect them.
E. Encourage suggestions for job improvements. Help employees to develop good suggestions. The suggestions can bring them recognition. The city's suggestion program offers additional encouragement through cash awards.

The supervisor who encourages employee participation is not surrendering his authority. He must still make decisions and initiate action, and he must continue to be ultimately responsible for the work of those he supervises. But, through employee participation, he is helping his group to develop greater ability and a sense of responsibility while getting the job done faster and better.

STEPS IN HANDLING A GRIEVANCE

1. Get the Facts
    a. Listen sympathetically
    b. Let him talk himself out
    c. Get his story straight
    d. Get his point of view
    e. Don't argue with him
    f. Give him plenty of time
    g. Conduct the interview privately
    h. Don't try to shift the blame or pass the buck

2. Consider the Facts
    a. Consider the employee's viewpoint
    b. How will the decision affect similar cases
    c. Consider each decision as a possible precedent
    d. Avoid snap judgments—don't jump to conclusions

3. Make or Get a Decision
    a. Frame an effective counter-proposal
    b. Make sure it is fair to all
    c. Have confidence in your judgment
    d. Be sure you can substantiate your decision

4. Notify the Employee of Your Decision
   Be sure he is told; try to convince him that the decision is fair and just.

5. Take Action When Needed and If Within Your Authority
   Otherwise, tell employee that the matter will be called to the attention of the proper person or that nothing can be done, and why it cannot.

6. Follow through to see that the desired result is achieved.

7. Record key facts concerning the complaint and the action taken.

8. Leave the way open to him to appeal your decision to a higher authority.

9. Report all grievances to your superior, whether they are appealed or not.

DISCIPLINE

Discipline is training that develops self-control, orderly conduct, and efficiency.

To discipline does not necessarily mean to punish.

To discipline does mean to train, to regulate, and to govern conduct.

I. THE DISCIPLINARY INTERVIEW

Most employees sincerely want to do what is expected of them. In other words, they are self-disciplined. Some employees, however, fail to observe established rules and standards, and disciplinary action by the supervisor is required.

The primary purpose of disciplinary action is to improve conduct without creating dissatisfaction, bitterness, or resentment in the process.

Constructive disciplinary action is more concerned with causes and explanations of breaches of conduct than with punishment. The disciplinary interview is held to get at the causes of apparent misbehavior and to motivate better performance in the future.

It is important that the interview be kept on an impersonal a basis as possible. If the supervisor lets the interview descend to the plane of an argument, it loses its effectiveness.

II. PLANNING THE INTERVIEW

Get all pertinent facts concerning the situation so that you can talk in specific terms to the employee.

Review the employee's record, appraisal ratings, etc.

Consider what you know about the temperament of the employee. Consider your attitude toward the employee. Remember that the primary requisite of disciplinary action is fairness.

Don't enter upon the interview when angry.

Schedule the interview for a place which is private and out of hearing of others.

III. CONDUCTING THE INTERVIEW

   A. Make an effort to establish accord.
   B. Question the employee about the apparent breach of discipline. Be sure that the question is not so worded as to be itself an accusation.
   C. Give the employee a chance to tell his side of the story. Give him ample opportunity to talk.
   D. Use understanding—listening except where it is necessary to ask a question or to point out some details of which the employee may not be aware. If the employee misrepresents facts, make a plain, accurate statement of the facts, but don't argue and don't engage in personal controversy.
   E. Listen and try to understand the reasons for the employee's (mis)conduct. First of all, don't assume that there has been a breach of discipline. Evaluate the employee's reasons for his conduct in the light of his opinions and feelings concerning the consistency and reasonableness of the standards which he was expected to follow. Has the supervisor done his part in explaining the reasons for the rule? Was the employee's behavior unintentional or deliberate? Does he think he had real reasons for his actions? What new facts is he telling? Do the facts justify his actions? What causes, other than those mentioned, could have stimulated the behavior?
   F. After listening to the employee's version of the situation, and if censure of his actions is warranted, the supervisor should proceed with whatever criticism is justified. Emphasis should be placed on future improvement rather than exclusively on the employee's failure to measure up to expected standards of job conduct.
   G. Fit the criticism to the individual. With one employee, a word of correction may be all that is required.
   H. Attempt to distinguish between unintentional error and deliberate misbehavior. An error due to ignorance requires training and not censure.
   I. Administer criticism in a controlled, even tone of voice, never in anger. Make it clear that you are acting as an agent of the department. In general, criticism should refer to the job or the employee's actions and not to the person. Criticism of the employee's work is not an attack on the individual.
   J. Be sure the interview does not destroy the employee's self-confidence. Mention his good qualities and assure him that you feel confident that he can improve his performance.
   K. Wherever possible, before the employee leaves the interview, satisfy him that the incident is closed, that nothing more will be said on the subject unless the offense is repeated.

www.ingramcontent.com/pod-product-compliance
Lightning Source LLC
Chambersburg PA
CBHW081815300426
44116CB00014B/2373